Research & Development Aircraft No.4

X-45

Uninhabited Combat Air Vehicle

Hugh Harkins

X-45

Uninhabited Combat Air Vehicle

© Hugh Harkins 2013

Published by Centurion Publishing
Glasgow
G65 9YE
United Kingdom

ISBN 10: 1-903630-21-5
ISBN 13: 978-1-903630-21-1

This volume first published in 2013

The Author is identified as the copyright holder of this work under sections 77 and 78 of the Copyright Designs and Patents Act 1988

Cover design © Centurion Publishing & Createspace

Page layout, concept and design © Centurion Publishing

All rights reserved. No part of this publication may be reproduced, stored in a retrieval system, transmitted in any form, or by any means, electronic, mechanical or photocopied, recorded or otherwise, without the written permission of the Publisher

The Publisher and Author would like to thank all companies and services for their assistance and contributions in the preparation of this publication

X-45

Uninhabited Combat Air Vehicle

Table of Contents

Chapter One: The Road to the Uninhabited Combat Air Vehicle   4

Chapter Two: Boeing X-45A Demonstrator   19

Chapter Three: Northrop Grumman X-47A Pegasus   75

Chapter Four: Joint-Uninhabited Combat Air System & Beyond   79

Chronology   85

Glossary   86

Preface

The X-45 was born from the studies of a number of programs in the 1990's aimed at producing technology that could be incorporated into a viable uninhabited air vehicle designed to autonomously conduct a range of operational missions including strike and suppression of enemy air defences. The successful conduct of the X-45 program paved the way for the new generation of Uninhabited Combat Air Vehicles being flight tested in the early part of the second decade of the 21st Century, including the Boeing Phantom Ray, which is a direct descendant of the X-45 Advanced Technology Demonstrators of the previous decade.

Chapter One

The Road to the Uninhabited Combat Air Vehicle

An X-45A drops a GPS-guided weapon in 2004. A decade before the concept of an autonomous purpose designed UCAV seemed a world from reality. Boeing

The operational deployment of UCAV's (Uninhabited Combat Air Vehicles) in strike roles "is going to be a reality. It is just a question of when." These were the words of the President of Lockheed Martin Aeronautics speaking in Canberra, Australia on 11 May 1999. As he was speaking, DARPA, Boeing and the USAF were pressing ahead with their efforts to fly and demonstrate two UCAV demonstrators by 2002.

In the 1990's, UAV (Uninhabited Air Vehicles) and UCAV became buzzwords as new advances in digital technology saw a number of UAV's enter service or development. However, the UAV/UCAV concepts were hardly new. As far back as the 19th Century crude air balloons were filled with explosives with the aim that they would descend behind an enemy's forward area and explode; with ineffective results. This method of

By the mid-1990's, larger. more sophisticated UAV's like the Lockheed Martin Darkstar emerged. Technology developed for these programs paved the way for future UAV programs. Lockheed Martin

attack was also tried by Japan during Word War II. While United States Army Air Force Boeing B-29 Superfortress bombers were firebombing Japanese cities using incendiary bombs. Japan tried to strike back; launching balloons with incendiary devices. The plan was that the high altitude jet stream winds encountered at altitudes in excess of 30,000-ft would blow the balloons across the Pacific and over the United States. A control system on the balloon was designed to allow the balloon to fly for around three days before initiating a gunpowder burn that would release bombs and ignite a fuse that would in theory destroy the balloon. Over 9,000 balloons, the first on 3 November 1944, were launched with hundreds confirmed as having reached the US with no less than 17 States having balloons fall on them. Balloons even reached the East Coast of the US as far as Texas and others fell on Canada and Mexico, the last falling in April 1945. The balloons caused some damage and killed a number of people, but were not very effective as a weapon system.

In Europe, a much more deadly and effective weapon system made its debut on 13 June 1944, just days after the allied landing on the Normandy Coast of France. The Fieseler Fi 103 V-1 Flying Bomb was used to attack southern England with devastating effect. Although ground defences and fighter aircraft shot many down, the V-1 menace was not removed until the allied armies overran launch sites in Europe. This weapon was also adapted for air launch from converted German bombers and used operationally.

The RQ-4A Global Hawk UAV was designed to have a degree of autonomy, although this was much less than that required for the UCAV program. USAF

In the second half of the 1990's a number of UCAV concepts were being defined. This Lockheed Martin concept was for a VTOL UCAV for operations from USN surface vessels. Lockheed Martin

Another German weapon system that could be classed as an early UCAV or cruise missile was the Mistel (Mistletoe), which took obsolete time-expired Junkers Ju 88A-4 bombers, which were converted into unmanned drones packed with an explosive warhead and mated to a fighter aircraft mounted above the bomber. The fighter would release the weapon, which would then descend towards the target. Later in the program new-build bombers were converted to Mistel on the production line. The allies also experimented with unmanned drones with varying degrees of success. UAV's were also used during the Korean War and more sophisticated UAV drones were used for reconnaissance during the Vietnam War. Missions flown by UAV's were at a much-reduced cost compared with manned flights and eliminated the risk to pilots completely.

During the 1960's and 70's, the USAF studied the potential of arming unmanned drones for a variety of roles ranging from SEAD (Suppression of Enemy Air Defences) to strike. However, no operational armed drones were fielded and interest waned along with interest in UAV's throughout the 1970's and early 1980's. While limited capability UAV's were fielded by some nations in the 1980's, particularly for the reconnaissance role, the revolution in interest in such systems was kick started in the wake of the 1991 Gulf War, when the handfuls of UAV's deployed performed better than expected, particularly at tactical level, providing commanders with intelligence when more expensive manned reconnaissance assets were heavily committed elsewhere.

Throughout the 1990's there was an explosion of UAV's designs, ranging from simple hand launched vehicles a few centimetres across to the huge Northrop Grumman RQ-4A Global Hawk designed for the strategic reconnaissance role.

Many programs that emerged in the late 1980's and early 1990's resulted in service entry of such systems as the General Atomics RQ-1A Predator; which entered USAF service and the IAI (Israeli Aircraft Industries) Hunter, which entered US Army service. Israel has also operated UAV's for a number of years and remains one of the world leaders in the design of UAV's.

Artist impression of a 1990's VTOL UCAV operating from a warship. The concept required the UCAV's to operate aircraft carriers down to smaller Frigate and Destroyer class surface combatants. Lockheed Martin

In the 1990's off the shelf inhabited combat aircraft were studied as possible candidates to be converted into first generation UCAV's. Mission technologies tied to interest the USAF in an uninhabited conversion of the A-10 Thunderbolt II (above), while Lockheed Martin offered the F-16 Long-Range Defender UCAV conversion of redundant F-16A airframes (upper right). By 1997 there were studies for the possible conversion of the F/A-18 Hornet (bottom right) as a USN first generation naval UCAV.
USAF, NASA Langley and USN

During the March to June 1999 Kosovo conflict, a number of UAV systems including the German Army operated Canadair CL-289, US Army operated IAI Hunter and the USAF operated General Atomics RQ-1A Predator were employed. Operations over Kosovo also highlighted the vulnerability of these systems with at least one Predator, one Hunter and a number of CL-289's shot down.

Overshadowed by the Kosovo conflict, at the same time Indian forces were involved in operations against Pakistan backed separatists in the disputed Kashmir region. During these operations, Indian forces employed UAV's on tactical reconnaissance duties and for counter bombardment of Pakistan artillery positions along the LOC (Line of Control). However, it was operations over Kosovo that saw the UAV directly involved in strike operations when USAF RQ-1A Predators were used to laser designate targets for strike aircraft, a role at first denied and then later admitted by the US DoD (Department of Defence).

Going into the second half of the 1990's, Northrop Grumman was studying UCAV designs which resembled a scaled down B-2 Bomber (above). This replaced the earlier UCAV iteration which featured a gull shaped wing (right): Northrop Grumman

With a military budget almost equivalent to that of the rest of the world combined, it is the United States that is taking the UAV to new horizons. Increasingly sophisticated and larger UAV's such as the Lockheed Martin Darkstar and the Teledyne Ryan (Northrop Grumman) RQ-4A Global Hawk emerged in the 1990's. Lessons learned from the success and failures of such programs led to renewed interest in the notion of an UCAV. While the Darkstar program was cancelled, the Global Hawk, despite the loss of a number of aircraft in development or operations, is now in service. The loss of the Global Hawks highlighted the dangers associated with flying UAV/UCAV's even with the sophistication incorporated into the Global Hawk. Sophisticated, as they were, Darkstar and Global Hawk paled in comparison to the difficulties associated with development of a viable autonomous UCAV system.

In the early 1990's, the notion of an autonomous reusable UCAV was viewed by many as science fiction. However, this decade would see enormous advances in technology, particularly the digital and information revolution, which would bring the idea of a viable UCAV system much closer to reality.

In 1992, the US ONR (Office of Naval Research) had provided funding for research into an uninhabited, manoeuvrable, reusable air vehicle, which would be a highly autonomous, armed weapon system known as the HMLV (Highly Manoeuvrable Lethal Vehicle). This program ran for four years with research indicating that huge cost savings, estimated at around 70% the cost of a piloted fighter aircraft, over a 20-year period could arise with adoption of such a system. The program concluded with the recommendation that further research into technology applicable to a future uninhabited armed air vehicle be conducted. Another recommendation was that less sophisticated armed air vehicles be built in the shorter term to allow experience to be gained in the operation of this new field of military technology.

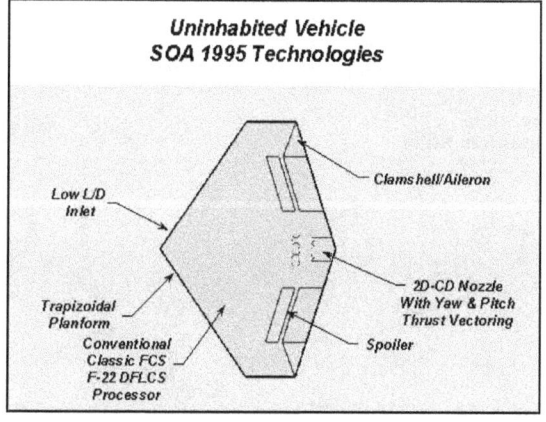

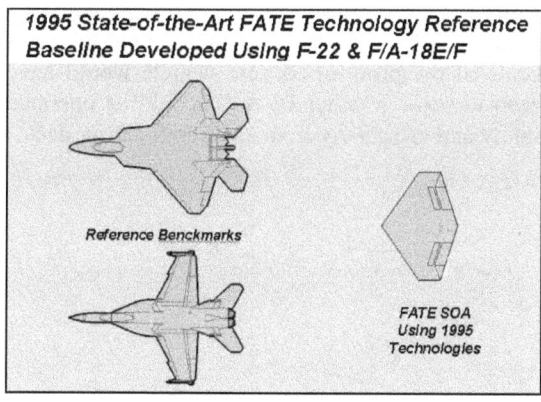

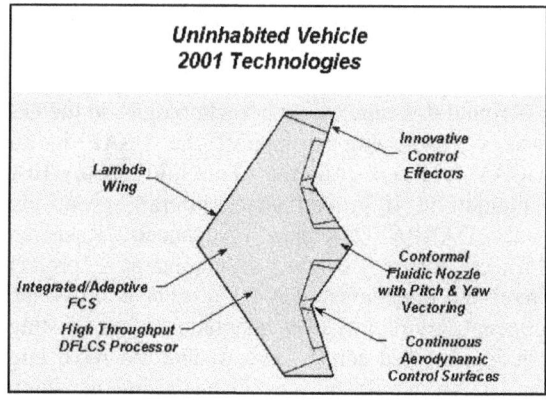

Top left: This design studied by Lockheed Martin in the 1990's, based on 1995 technologies, incorporated a tailless trapezoidal planform with clamshell ailerons and a 2-D pitch and yaw thrust-vectoring nozzle. The vehicle would have incorporated technology used in the F-22 Raptor, including the FCS (Flight Control System). Centre left: This chart shows the 1995 technology derived UCAV small size compared with the F-22 Raptor and F/A-18E/F Super Hornet inhabited tactical fighters then in development. Bottom left: 1990's UCAV technologies projected forward to 2001 showed the move from the 1995 trapezoidal wing to the lambda wing, incorporation of an integrated adaptive flight control system, innovative control effectors and conformal fluidic pitch and yaw thrust-vectoring. Lockheed Martin

Above: This mid-1990's artist impression shows UCAV's and inhabited combat aircraft based on a common airframe operating in mixed formations.

A 1996/97 research-effort studied concepts for low-cost tactical UCAV's. One concept was the JSAAWS (Joint-Semi-Autonomous Weapon System), which helped pave the way for later progress in the field of a UCAV suitable for naval operations. It was estimated that the JSAAWS could be between a quarter and half the size of a McDonnell Douglas (now Boeing) F/A-18 Hornet fighter and in mid-1997 the USN was looking along the lines of a STOL (Short Take-Off and Landing) vehicle.

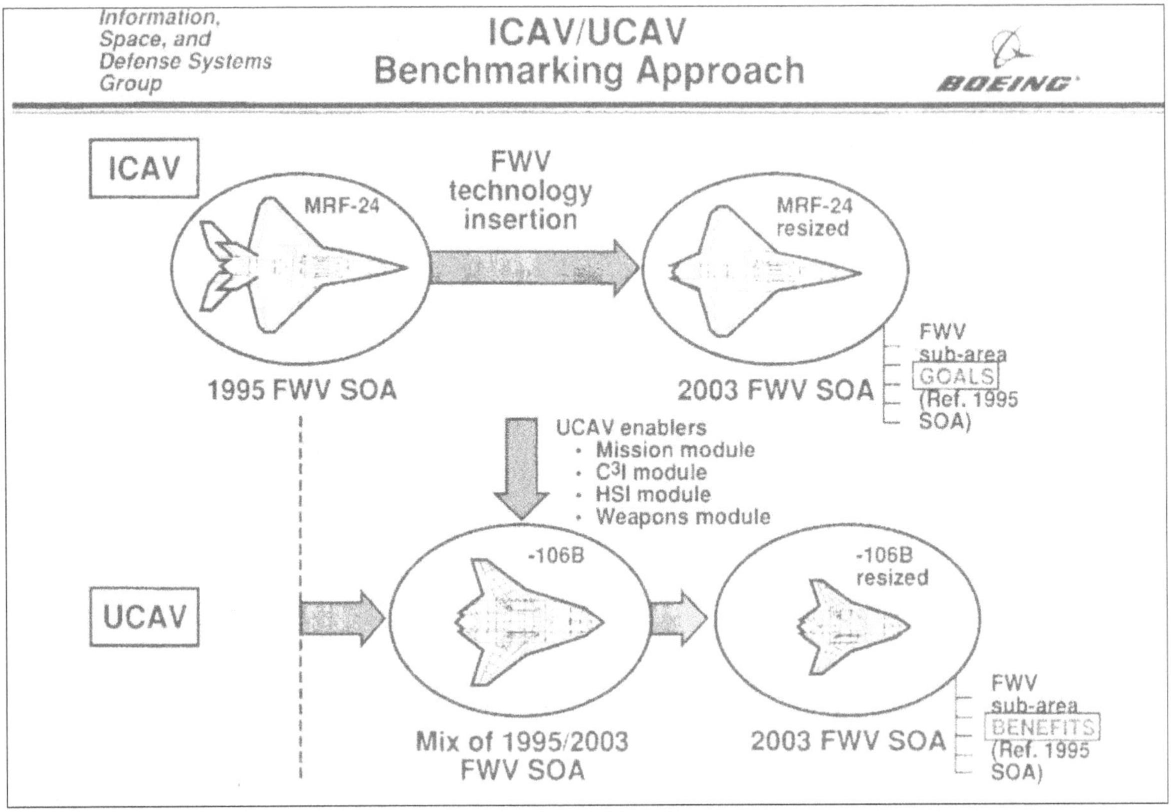

ICAV/UCAV Benchmarking Approach

Information, Space, and Defense Systems Group — BOEING

In the mid-1990's, Boeing conducted studies into technology applicable to both ICAV (Inhabited Combat Air Vehicles) and UCAV's under the FWV (Fixed Wing Vehicle) program. The UCAV Model-106B was studied with 1995 technologies and resized for a projected 2003 UCAV. Boeing

In August 1997, the USN announced that it planned to award Lockheed Martin Tactical Aircraft Systems a sole-source contract to conduct design analysis of an UNSA (Uninhabited Naval Strike Aircraft) before the end of the year. The USN was by this time seriously thinking along the lines of fielding a survivable tactical uninhabited platform for dangerous strike missions. The UNSA would have been required to have vertical/short take-off-and-landing capabilities. Under the terms of the contract it was understood that Lockheed Martin would be asked to develop three UNSA concepts capable of operating from aircraft carriers and other warships.

At the same time the USN was considering adopting the F/A-18 Hornet as the basis for a next-generation UCAV. This uninhabited F/A-18 study was being conducted alongside the other studies, which would consider a host of UCAV concepts, an "air-arsenal ship" and a replacement for the Boeing F/A-18E/F Super Hornet being developed as the USN's future strike fighter. One of the main goals of the proof-of-concept vehicle would have been to show whether UCAV's could be operated safely and effectively from an aircraft carrier deck.

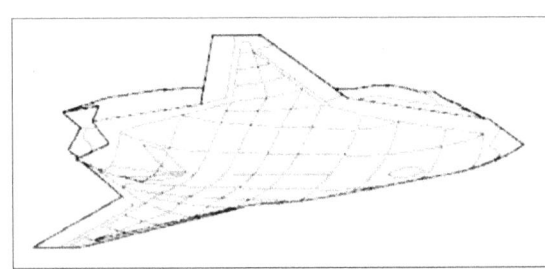

This concept shows the layout of a Boeing Model-106B UCAV in 1997. Boeing

Around this time Mission Technologies in the US was vainly trying to interest the USAF in an UCAV variant of the Fairchild A/OA-10A Thunderbolt II ground attack aircraft, proposing that DARPA (Defence Advanced Research Projects Agency) conduct a demonstration project involving the converted A-10 in order to prove the concept; arguing that the adaptation of an existing tried and tested combat aircraft like the A-10 into an UCAV would be a solid beginning to 'jump start' more advanced UCAV programs.

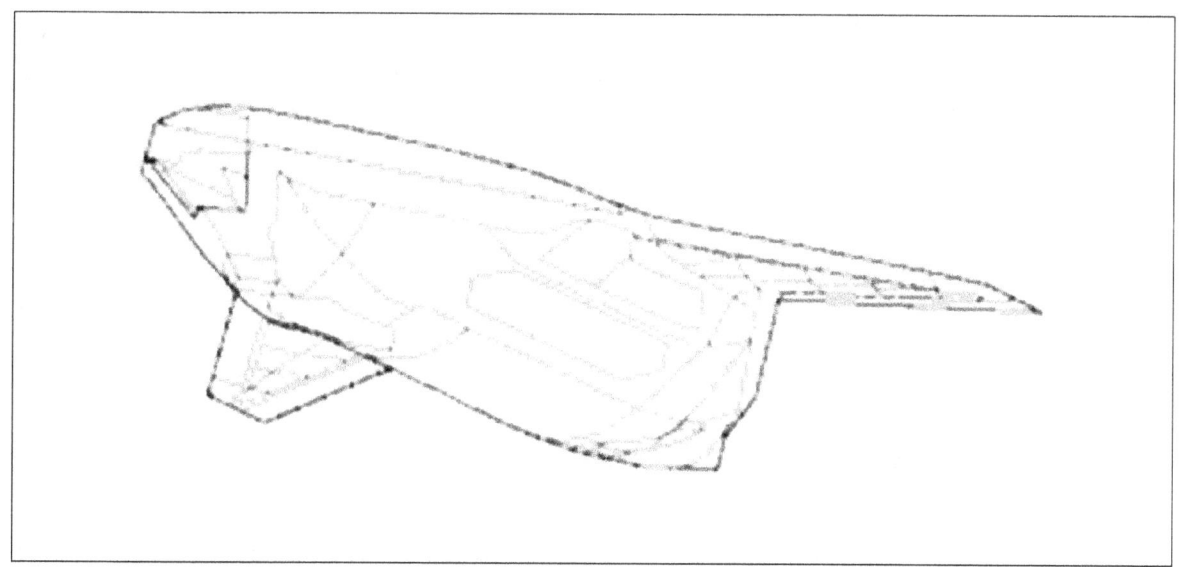

This view of the Boeing Model-106B notional UCAV shows a resemblance to the fuselage adopted for the later Boeing X-32 Joint Strike Fighter technology demonstrator. The Model-106B UCAV design featured two internal weapons bays mounted in the deep fuselage. Boeing

Lockheed Martin had offered an interim UCAV based on its F-16 fighter aircraft. This conversion, initially known as the F-16 Long Endurance Defender, would have seen the F-16A's low aspect ratio wing replaced by a thick high aspect ratio wing 60-ft in length and similar to the Fairchild A-10. A planned endurance of up to eight hours would have been achieved through more efficient aerodynamics and a 22,000-lb fuel capacity, with additional fuel housed in a tank in the space previously occupied by the cockpit. The 20-mm Vulcan cannon and associated ammunition feed and storage would have been removed with the space being allocated to additional datalink and communications equipment.

In mid-1997, Northrop Grumman revealed its own UCAV design, which company officials claimed could be deployed within 15 years to handle "dull, dirty and dangerous missions". Acknowledging its UCAV research, Northrop Grumman's military-aircraft-systems division at El Segundo, California, revealed the design of a low-cost, stealthy; re-usable, double-delta planform/gull-winged UCAV, which would be about half the size of inhabited fighter aircraft. Northrop Grumman stated that this was only one example of the UCAV design work then being carried out and that the UCAV onboard sensors would generate target information for the remotely situated mission controller, who would authorise the UCAV to release 225-kg or 450-kg bombs.

In 1997, Boeing conducted studies evaluating potential benefits of advanced technologies, which were then proposed for development under the notional FWV (Fixed Wing Vehicle) program for future fighter/attack aircraft. Technologies for ICAV (Inhabited Combat Air Vehicle) and UCAV notional vehicles were studied. The ICAV portion studied technologies relative to an F-22 reference aircraft. However, as F-22 data was classified, Boeing used an aircraft model known as the MRF-24 with a single F-22 class engine. The UCAV segment of the FWV used a reference UCAV developed under Boeings IRAD (Internal Research and Development) program, which incorporated advanced technologies, in advance of those used in the F-22 Raptor. These included tailless design and pitch/yaw thrust vectoring.

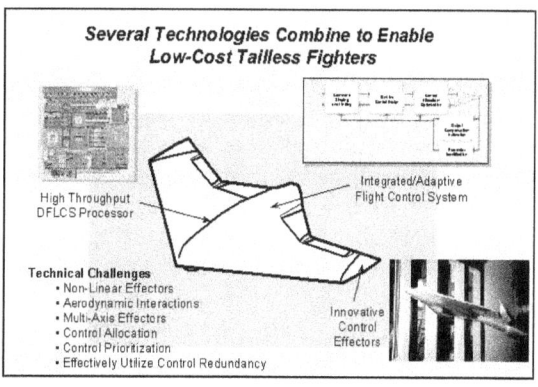

This chart shows technology being developed in the 1990's to enable viable tailless fighter aircraft, including UCAV's, to be developed. Lockheed Martin

This retouched photograph depicts the scene at a USAF air base with operational UCAV's. Northrop Grumman

The UCAV reference was designated UCAV Model-106B. This design evolved from a number of previous UCAV configurations under development by Boeing. The vehicle was tailless and was designed to carry a payload of two JDAM's in internal weapons bays. A multi-axis thrust vectoring system was incorporated providing the vehicle with pitch and yaw control. The vehicle design incorporated an afterburning turbofan engine of medium bypass ratio based on the engine core of the F-22's F119. While not designed to have supersonic dash speed or be as manoeuvrable as the MRF-24F ICAV, the Model-106B was designed to have a near 23-degrees per second maximum instantaneous turn rate, a 13 degrees per second sustained turn rate and a high subsonic maximum speed. Much of the design technology developed in the MRF-24 and Model-106B programs fed into Boeings UCAV program in the late 1990's.

The X-45 program has its roots in DARPA plans announced in October 1997 to demonstrate an UCAV capable of air-defence suppression and mobile-target attack. This was the first major UCAV programme to be officially launched. The program would be conducted under an ATD (Advanced Technology Demonstration) conducted by DARPA and the USAF. The aim of the program was to develop and demonstrate technologies for an affordable UCAV system, which could be fielded by the USAF around 2010.

In the 1990's, Lockheed Martin studied concepts for a submarine launched UCAV, which would be launched while the submarine was still submerged. Lockheed Martin

This artist impression of a Northrop Grumman UCAV concept released in the late 1990's bore a resemblance to the design that eventually emerged as the X-47B developed under the J-UCAS & later UCAS-D program. Northrop Grumman

The UCAV program took a major step forward on 16 April 1998 when DARPA and the USAF selected four contractor teams to participate in the Phase 1 TDP (Technology Demonstration Program). Each team received $4 million contracts for the initial 10-month study, analysis and preliminary design phase. The selected contractor team leads were Lockheed Martin Tactical Aircraft Systems, Northrop Grumman, Raytheon and Boeing.

The goal of this joint DARPA/USAF UCAV technology demonstration program was to demonstrate the technical feasibility for an UCAV system, which could effectively and safely prosecute SEAD and strike missions at an affordable cost. The US Department of Defence provided specific mission objectives and guidance on overall system capability to the contractors and each team conducted mission effectiveness and affordability trades to optimise an operational system design before defining an UCAV demonstrator system to validate the critical technologies.

DARPA estimated that a massive reduction in operating costs would result by fielding UCAV's. Estimates suggested that operating and support costs could be reduced by as much as 80% over an existing fighter such as the Lockheed Martin F-16 Fighting Falcon. This would be achieved through a number of means including reduced flight hours and maintenance personnel requirements. While about 80% of a piloted aircrafts service life is expended in training, and 20% in combat and operations, the proportions would be reversed for a UCAV. Most of the training would be performed in simulators and the vehicles would spend most of their lives in storage. UCAV's could, therefore, be designed for fewer flying hours, say 2,000 hours over 20 years compared with 8,000 hours for an inhabited fighter aircraft.

As originally envisioned, UCAV's were much smaller than the X-45C and X-47B vehicles developed under the J-UCAS program. This computer-generated image shows a 1990's concept for a USN UCAV. Northrop Grumman

In late 1998, Lockheed Martin stated that it was discontinuing work on the DARPA/USAF UCAV program leaving Boeing, Northrop Grumman and Raytheon Systems to compete for the contract. It was stated that Lockheed Martin's approach to the programme did not match DARPA requirements. Despite this announcement, Lockheed Martin continued work on other UCAV programs.

During the first phase of the program, the remaining three industry teams completed mission effectiveness and affordability trades to optimise their operational system design, identified critical technologies and issues and planned their Phase II demonstration programs.

The design of the Boeing UCAV drew on technology developed and flight tested during the 1990's. These included the subscale uninhabited X-36 and the piloted Boeing BoP (Bird of Prey); both tailless designs, a feature carried over to the X-45.

During the 1999 Kosovo conflict, the USAF converted a number of RQ-1A Predator UAV's to be capable of designating targets for tactical aircraft operating with laser guided bombs. USAF

The McDonnell Douglas (later Boeing) X-36, unveiled on 19 March 1996, was a 28% scale remotely piloted fighter design powered by a single 3.1- kN (700-lb) thrust William's F112 turbojet engine originally developed for the McDonnell Douglas AGM-129 Advanced Cruise Missile.

Control surfaces on the X-36 consisted of all-moving canard fore-planes, split ailerons and

Top: The Boeing Bird of Prey. Above: The McDonnell Douglas (later Boeing) X-36. Boeing and NASA DFRC

flaperons on the aft set wing. Three ailerons were mounted on the trailing edge of the wing, which was sharply cranked towards mid-span increasing the aircraft's low observable characteristics. The two outboard sections functioned independently and split to provide yaw control (using drag) while the inner section acted like a 'typical flaperon', the ailerons raising and lowering asymmetrically for pitch and roll control.

The aircraft's advanced single channel Honeywell developed Matrix-X digital auto-code FBW (Fly-By-Wire FCS (Flight Control System) was developed with commercially available components and was used in the McDonnell Douglas DC-XA and later adopted for the F-15 ACTIVE (Active Control Technology for Integrated Vehicles). The FBW FCS integrated control inputs using the split ailerons and a thrust-vectoring control system provided yaw control to compensate for the absent tail surfaces. The thrust-vector nozzle provided the initial control input until its limits were reached; at which point the split ailerons gradually took over. The thrust-vectoring system was based on a design developed by MDC in the late 1980's. The exhaust gases exit through a flattened exhaust nozzle, which is recessed slightly beneath the aircraft's broad 'beaver' tail.

Although thrust-vectoring control was a key element of the X-36 design, because the X-36 was designed to be tailless from the beginning the design philosophy did not actually require thrust vectoring to control the aircraft, therefore, it was still flyable in the event of a thrust-vectoring nozzle lockup or other failure.

A pilot controller in a virtual cockpit-complete with HUD (Head-Up Display) in a ground station flew the X-36, with a video camera mounted in the nose of the aircraft providing the ground station crew with a forward view from the aircraft. The man in-the-loop approach eliminated the need for an expensive and complex autonomous flight control system.

The first and only one of the two X-36 vehicles to fly during the program took to the air for the first time on 17 May 1997 and the last flight of the initial program was conducted on 12 November 1997, by which time the X-36 had flown 31 times and achieved an altitude of 20,500-ft and an AoA (Angle of Attack) of 40-degrees.

The low key end to the X-36 program and the fact that the latest US tactical fighter program, the Lockheed Martin F-35 Lightning II (Joint Strike Fighter), was designed with conventional vertical tails does not signal a waning of interest in tailless fighter designs. What does, however, seem likely is that the UCAV's will be at the forefront of future tailless tactical aircraft design. These vehicles will in all probability remain subsonic, at least in the near term and will not require the levels of agility that inhabited fighters require for combat manoeuvring. That said UCAV's will be required to be manoeuvrable enough to take evasive action and to avoid collisions in dense air traffic control airspace.

The Future Aircraft Technology Enhancement (FATE) program was launched with the aim of achieving quantum leaps in technology, which could be applied to future military and commercial aircraft. In the late 1990's it was speculated that the FATE program would receive the designation X-39. However, no designation was applied and the X-39 designation has not as yet been allocated.

The following data comes from a 1997 FATE report:

"Examples of FATE technologies include affordable low-observable data systems, active aero-elastic wing, robust composite sandwich structures, advanced compact inlets, photonic vehicle management systems, self-adaptive flight controls and electric actuation." Both Boeing and Lockheed performed a long-range study on next-generation aircraft.

A subset of the notional Fixed Wing Vehicle (FWV) Program, FATE was structured with three phases:

- **FATE I, Phase I: Define a set of aircraft technologies that must be flight test validated in a new air vehicle to meet FWV Phase I program goals for a fighter attack class of aircraft, including both inhabited and uninhabited aircraft.**
- **FATE I, Phase II: Develop preliminary vehicle design concepts, a demonstrator system, and demonstration plans.**
- **FATE II: Develop, build and flight-test a demonstrator vehicle to achieve program goals."**

FATE I, Phase I was used as a jump-start for the Uninhabited Combat Air Vehicle Advanced Technology Demonstration (UCAV ATD) X-45 that effectively replaced the FATE program, which studied the major benefits of tailless aircraft, design. In the past, tailless aircraft directional control has been provided by spoilers or drag rudders. This was done to de-couple the control system as much as possible. Unfortunately, spoilers and drag rudders have high attendant actuator requirements (a result of large hinge moments) and provide inadequate control power at high AoA.

"With quantum advances in throughput capabilities of digital processors, it is now possible to take advantage of advanced integrated/adaptive flight control techniques that make a decoupled control effector a requirement. As a result, more efficient aerodynamic controls, like the all-moving wing tip or spoiler-slot-deflector, can now be used for tailless aircraft lateral-directional control. Integration of these effectors reduces control suite weight fraction 5%, reduces hydraulic power requirements 45% (because hinge moments are much less than those of conventional surfaces), and vastly improves high AoA flying qualities. All of these factors contribute to improved agility.

Advanced flight control technologies that enable these unconventional effectors also reduce FCS complexity and cost and will reduce loss-of-control related accidents and mission-critical vulnerability."

Benefits of the various tailless technologies include

- Reduced drag (compared to a tailed airplane), reduced weight (compared to a 1995 SOA tail-less aircraft).
- Improved high-AoA agility and flying qualities.
- Reduced actuator redundancy requirements.
- Reduced number of Operational Flight Program (OFP) design cycles.
- Reduced control-related accidents and mission-critical vulnerability.

The last three improvements are attributable to the integrated/adaptive controls technologies rather than the innovative control effectors.

These improvements would be available to any configuration employing this type of flight control system, not just tailless aircraft. Finally, the enabler for all of these technologies is the new high-throughput processor now available for the flight control computer.

Drag Reduction Potential of Tailless Designs

Minimum drag data for two configurations employing vertical tails shows that the vertical tail accounts for 5% to 10% of the total airplane minimum drag at a cruise Mach number of 0.9. Configuration features like area distribution and interference affects results in variation of the tail contribution. Nevertheless, 5% CDmin is still significant.

Data from low-speed wind tunnel tests conducted during the Innovative Control Effectors (ICE) program show that the all-moving wing tip provides substantial yawing moments through 90-degrees AoA. The magnitude of the yaw power available is sufficient to provide Level 1 flying qualities to this vehicle. The high AoA directional control power available is superior to that available from vertical tail/rudder controls, which greatly improves agility levels. Together with multi-axis thrust vectoring, innovative controls can provide tailless aircraft with full envelope control, including unparalleled high AoA agility.

All-Moving Wing Tips and Spoiler-Slot-Deflectors Are Weight-Efficient Tailless Controls

An efficiency parameter was computed by dividing the control power available (DCn) by the weight of the effector and its actuator. The clamshell, typically used by previous tailless aircraft, has good weight efficiency at low dynamic pressure conditions. However, the high hinge moments associated with this control contribute to very poor high-speed efficiency. Furthermore, at high AoA, flow separation causes adverse roll-yaw characteristics that limit the usefulness of this surface during roll co-ordination. Both the all-moving wing tip and the spoiler-slot-deflector exhibit much smaller high-speed hinge moments, and are more efficient than the clamshell. A rudder has excellent weight efficiency throughout the majority of the AoA envelope, but suffers at high AoA as it loses effectiveness. At low speeds (low dynamic pressures), TV is the most efficient of any of the effectors. However, thrust vectoring control effectiveness falls off rapidly at high dynamic pressures, and its efficiency suffers. The all-moving wing tip provides good weight efficiency in all flight conditions (although not the best at any given one) and, therefore, is a good choice for tailless aircraft control. The spoiler-slot-deflector ranks second in this regard. Note that weight efficiency is as good as that of the F-16 rudder in the high-speed low-AoA condition.

Tailless Aircraft Risks/Penalties Compared with Those of Tailed Aircraft

There are also penalties and risks to be addressed when designing tailless aircraft when compared to conventional tailed aircraft. Penalties of choosing a tailless configuration include:

- Increased structural weight - A vertical tail and rudder are still the most weight efficient directional control and stabilisation device for most of the flight envelope.
- Increased hydraulic power requirements - Primarily this increase is caused by increased actuator rate requirements of the innovative effectors.
- Increased FCS complexity. A tailless design incorporating innovative controls drives the configuration to include the integrated/adaptive flight control algorithms to mitigate the complexity involved with using traditional control design philosophies.

Integration of innovative controls may compromise wing camber design on some configurations. This depends on planform and mission, and applies to wings having no leading-edge flaps. Note that the spoiler-slot-deflector controls do not carry this penalty."

As mentioned above, FATE Phase I was used as a launch platform for the (UCAV ATD, which eventually became the X-45A with this program eventually replacing the FATE program. The X-45 itself could trace its design lineage back to the Boeing Bird of Prey and the X-36, with design elements of both being incorporated.

As well as the X-45 and later UCAV-N, J-UCAS and UCAS-D programs, several other UCAV programs have emerged, with some falling by the wayside and others leading to further research program. Lockheed Martin received a six-month USN contract to define a family of UCAV's which could be launched from ships and submarines to attack high-value fixed targets or conduct SEAD missions within a range of 1,100-km (600-nm). Under the six month USN contract, Lockheed Martin was defining three notional UCAV UNSA (Uninhabited Naval Strike Aircraft) concepts. The three included STOVL and Vertical-Attitude Take-off and Landing (VATOL) which would be suitable for surface vessel launch and recovery. Most of the designs studied incorporated either full or quasi-tailless configurations.

Not long after the X-45 rollout in September 2000, the French manufacturer Dassault shocked its competitors by revealing that it had flight-tested a sub-scale, tailless UCAV demonstrator during July 2000. Dassault revealed that the vehicle was controlled using three flaperons on each wing. Several programs have emerged from underway in Europe including the French AVE and a BAE Systems design.

Other research platforms are contributing to the development of technology designed to enhance the operationally capability of a tailless agile fighter, which could be applicable to inhabited or uninhabited vehicles. Among these is the Boeing F-15 ACTIVE (Active Control for Integrated Vehicles), which on April 24, 1996 performed the first supersonic yaw thrust vectoring manoeuvre. Research into tailless flight for future fighter designs both piloted and uninhabited was also conducted on the surviving Rockwell (now Boeing) DASA (now EADS Germany) X-31A under the VECTOR (Vectoring Extremely short take-off and landing Control and Tailless operation Research) program

Chapter Two

Boeing X-45A Demonstrator

The first of 2 X-45A's, AV-1, sits outside the hanger at St Louis, Missouri following its official rollout in September 2000. Boeing

Although studies began in 1998, the X-45A program proper was born on 24 March 1999, when DARPA and the USAF selected Boeing to continue into Phase 2 of the UCAV ATD. Under the $131 million cost-share effort, Boeing was to develop two vehicles, a re-configurable mission control station and appropriate supportability elements to demonstrate the key technologies, operational capabilities and affordability benefits of integrating UCAV's into inhabited air operations. The contract called for Boeing to build and flight-test a demonstration system by 2002. Boeing Seattle was responsible for the mission control system and overall program management, whereas the St. Louis location had the lead for the air vehicle segment. NASA DFRC was also involved in the UCAV program, finalising its technical task agreements with Boeing in 1999. Dryden also provided the operational location for the X-45A test program as well technical expertise.

The Boeing phase 2 UCAV concept, which received the designation X-45A, was designed to exploit real-time on-board and off-board sensors to quickly detect identify and locate fixed, re-locatable and mobile targets. Secure communications and advanced cognitive decision aids would provide a human operator with the situational awareness and positive air vehicle control necessary to authorise munitions release.

Above and right: Once Phase IIA of the DARPA/USAF program got underway a number of artist impressions of Boeings UCAV concept appeared. Both concepts are shown releasing munitions from the internal weapons bays. Like a number of other UCAV concepts the Boeing approach included a stealthy tailless design capable of a high degree of autonomous operation. Boeing

The ATD program would also demonstrate the potential for future UCAV systems to fully exploit the emerging information revolution. It would take advantage of multiple, real-time data sources and secure communication networks to plan for and respond to, the dynamically changing battlefield. They program would exploit the additional design and operational freedoms provided by removing the pilot from the vehicle to achieve a new paradigm in aircraft affordability and supportability.

The X-45A system would include a stealthy, tailless 27-ft long, 8,000-lb (empty) vehicle with a 34-ft wingspan. The vehicles had a re-configurable mission control system with robust satellite-relay and line-of-site communications links for distributed control in all air combat situations; and a supportability approach that included long-term, compact storage, periodic systems testing and re-assembly for flight in just over one hour.

The demonstrators were powered by a single Honeywell F124-GA-100 non-afterburning turbofan engine rated at 28-kN, which was apparently not visible from the frontal aspect. Air was supplied to the engine via a notched serpentine air intake at the front of the vehicle and the exhaust featured a two-dimensional low observable yaw-thrust-vectoring nozzle, which was fully integrated with the aircraft's flight control system. Thrust vectoring was used in lieu of vertical tails, drawing on experience gained during the X-36 program.

The X-45 flight vehicles during final assembly, and loading onto a Boeing C-17 for transportation in their storage containers. All DARPA

The first X-45A, AV-1 undergoes wing structural mode integration testing at St Louis. DARPA

The X-45A flight-vehicles incorporated shaping to reduce radar signature, but did not incorporate RAM (Radar Absorbent Material). The swept wing X-45A is of composite construction with a foam matrix core and a composite fibre reinforced epoxy skin. The vehicle is tailless, with no vertical tail and features a low-set wing and blended fuselage with a straight leading edge and a 'W' shaped planform trailing edge. The vehicles have two internal weapons bays allowing stores and test equipment to be carried internally enhancing the stealthy shape. During testing one bay was fully operational, while the second bay was used to house an avionics pallet. An internal fuel load of 1220-kg could be carried and payload was 680-kg.

The vehicles were all electric with the exception of the nose-wheel steering and braking system. The undercarriage consists of a fully retractable tricycle-gear with single main-wheel units and a single nose-wheel. The vehicles were designed to be air transportable, with detachable wings for ease of loading. For transport the X-45A was packed into a container; an integral part of the UCAV concept. Up to 6 X-45A sized UCAV's could be carried by a single Boeing C-17A transport aircraft.

X-45A AV-1 is seen in the assembly hanger at St Louis. The vehicles' port wing is being attacked to the fuselage. The starboard wing is already in place. DARPA

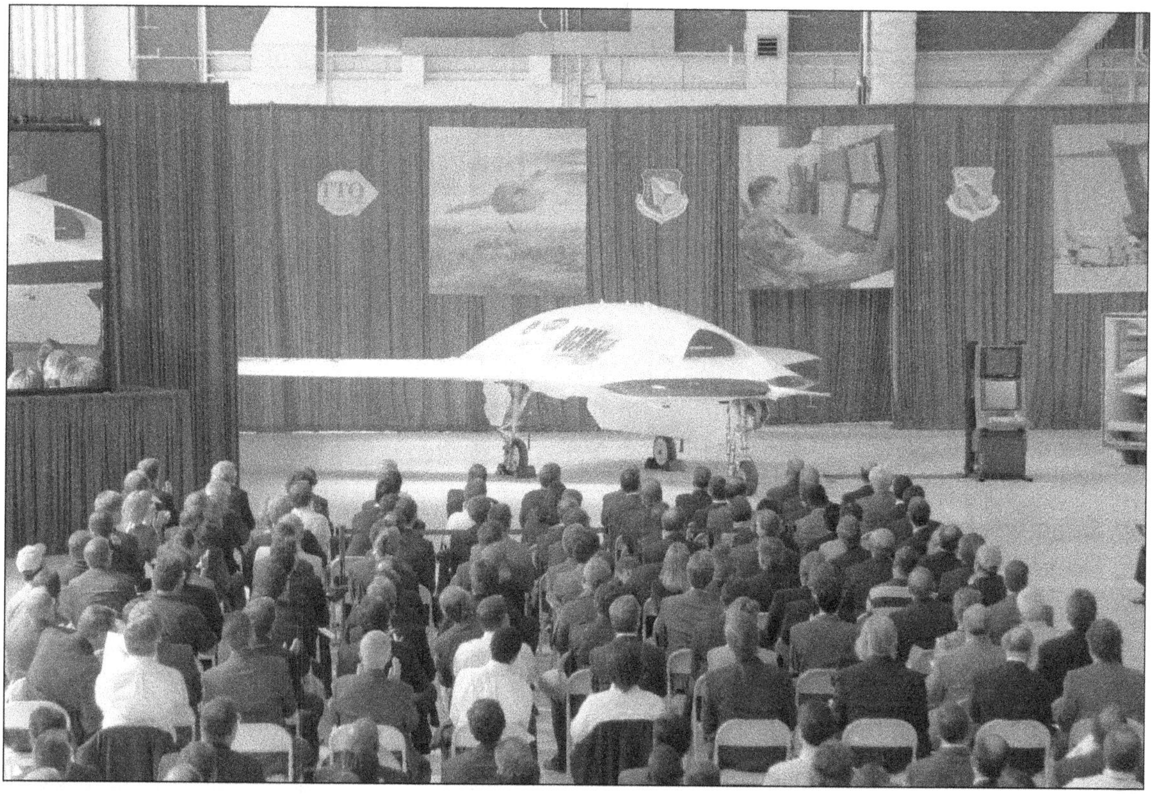

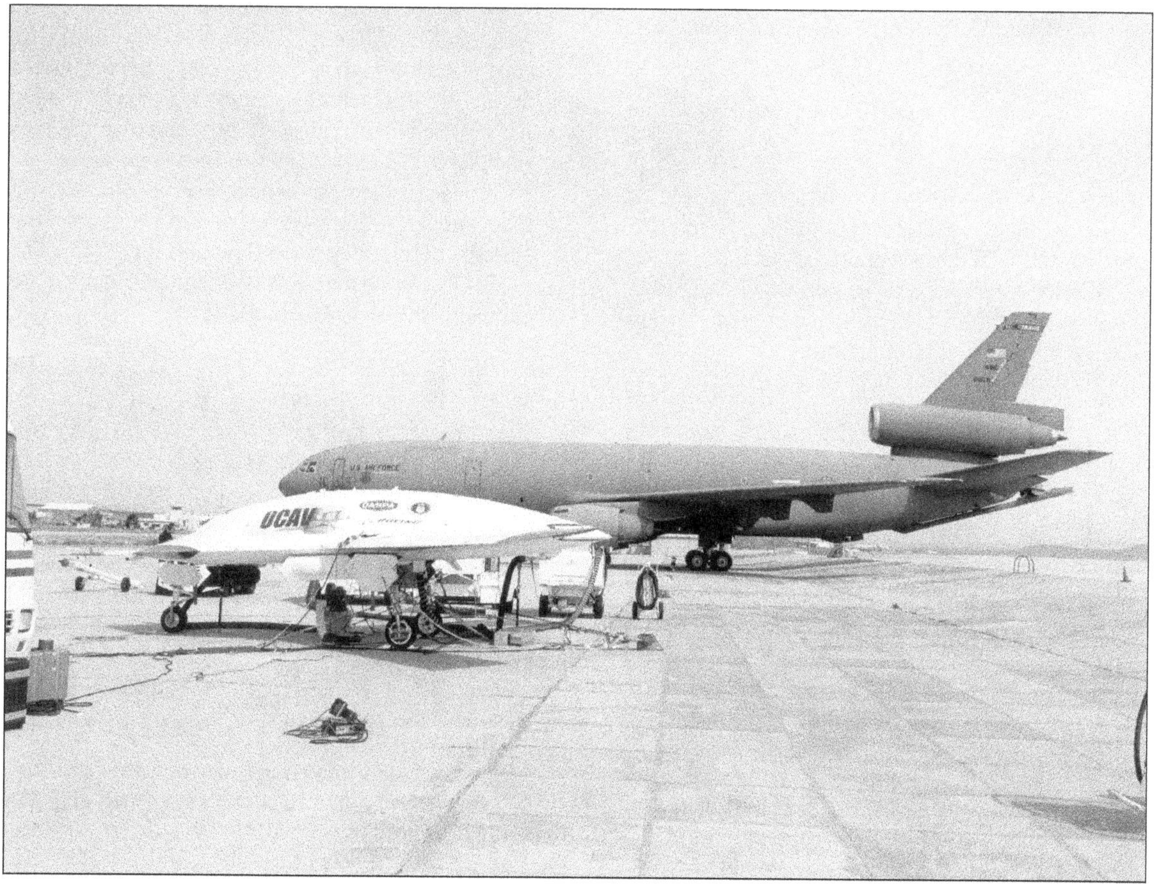
UCAV

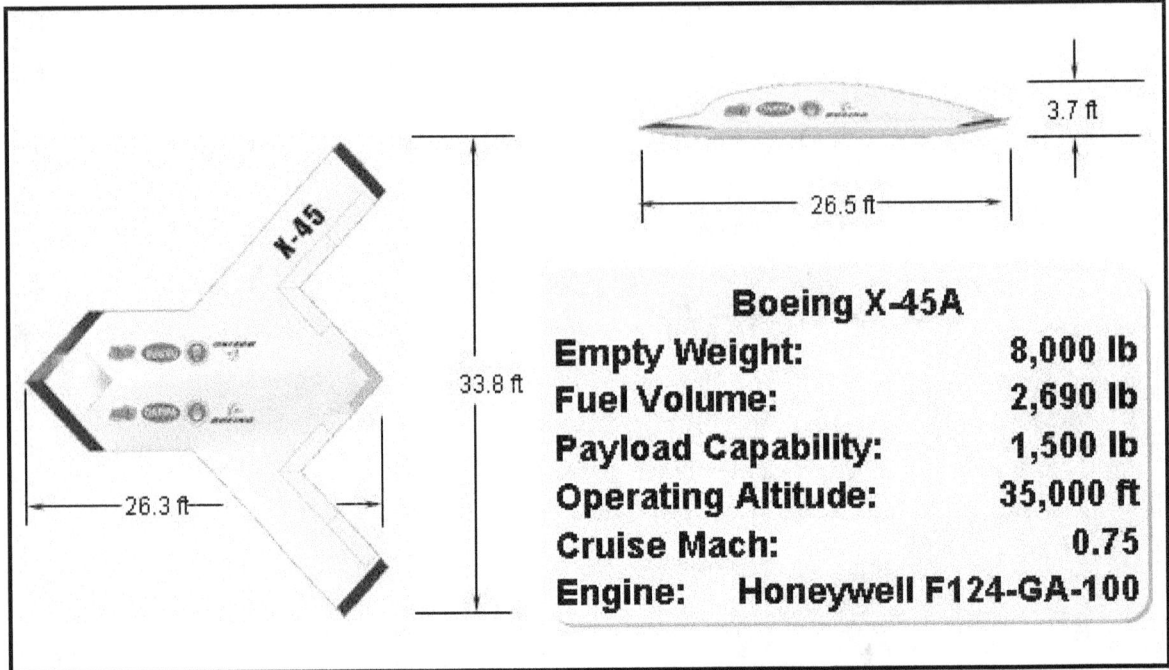

Previous page top: Once structurally complete the first X-45A, AV-1, was unveiled in a ceremony at Boeings St Louis facility in September 2000. Boeing
Previous page bottom: AV-1 is prepared for electromagnetic interference testing at Edwards AFB. DARPA

Above: General arrangement 3-view drawing of the X-45A. DARPA

The X-45A was designed with a high degree of autonomy. Safety features included a return to home feature, whereby, if at any given time during the mission the vehicle experienced "specific failures" then the X-45A would autonomously abort the mission and return to base.

The X-45A vehicles themselves were only a part of the UCAV system; this also included storage shipping containers and ground control segments. Command and control of the X-45A vehicles was conducted through a duel-display console housed in an environmentally controlled shelter, which was trailer-based. The X-45 program also utilised a Lockheed T-33 jet trainer, which was to act as a UCAV surrogate to conduct some flight-testing independent of the X-45A's and to flight-test some systems before they were flown on the X-45A. The T-33 UCAV surrogate was operated from Dryden alongside the X-45A vehicles.

This head-on view shows the compact lines of the X-45A. DARPA

Following X-45A AV-1's delivery to Edwards AFB in November 2000, the vehicle began a series of ground testing including weapons loading demonstrations, which were conducted on 21 May 2001. DARPA

The X-45A shape was designed with stealth features in mind. However, the demonstrators did not incorporate any radar absorbent materials in their construction. The lack of any vertical tail surfaces also enhanced the low-observable qualities of the vehicle. The incorporation of a thrust-vector control system compensated for the lack of tail control surfaces found on conventional aircraft design. The serpentine air intake at the front of the vehicle fed air to the engine, which it is understood was visible from the frontal aspect further enhancing the stealth qualities of the design. DARPA

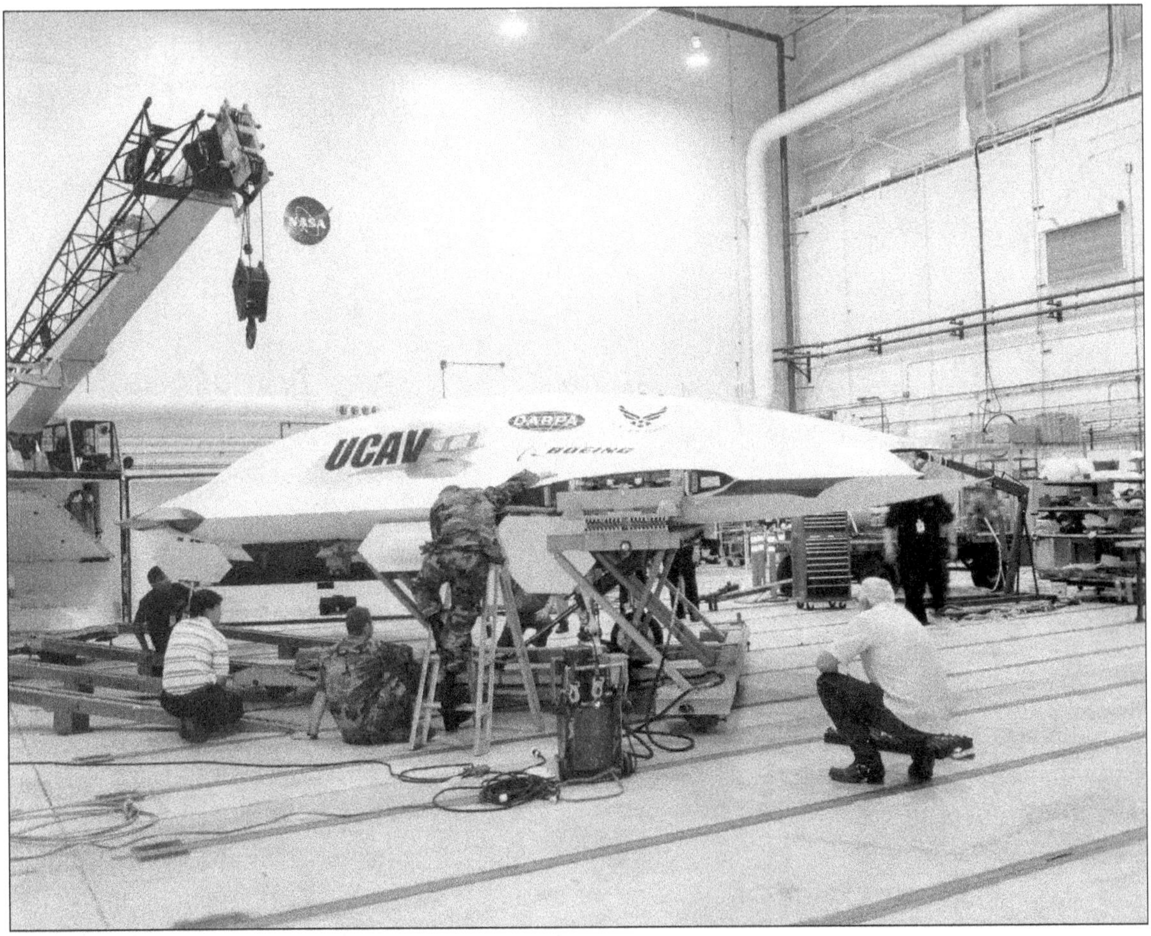
UCAV
DARPA
BOEING

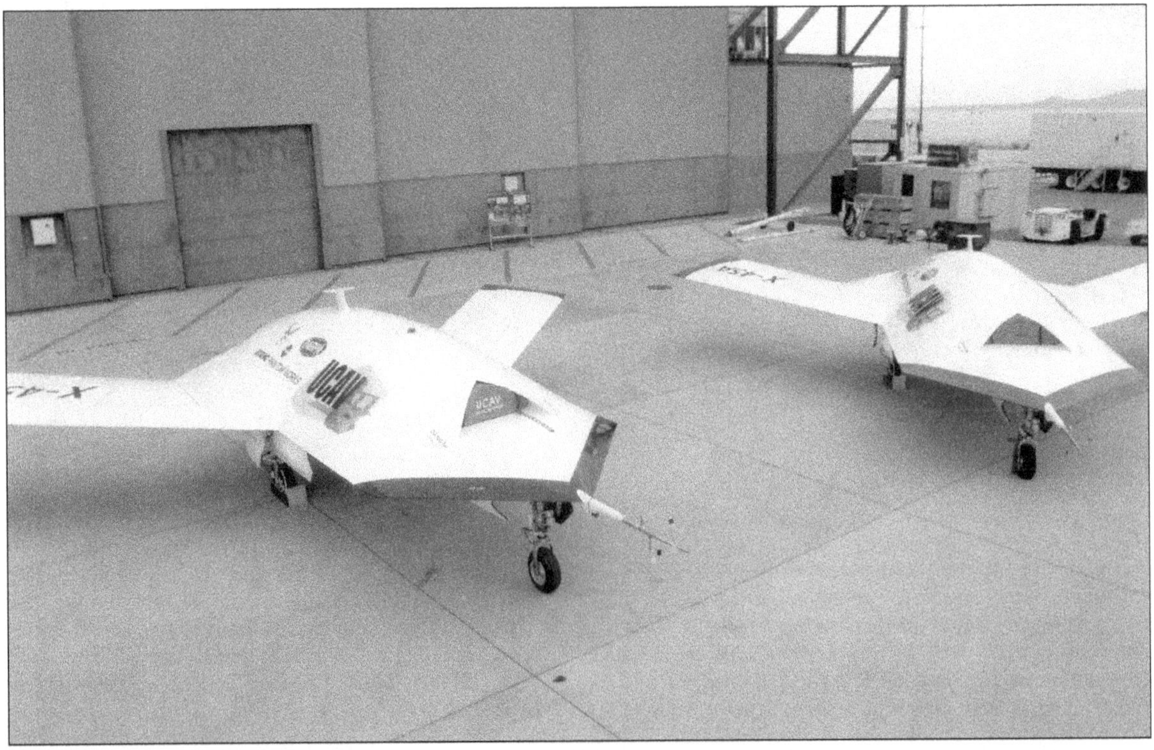
UCAV

Previous page top: The second X-45A, AV-2, on stilts on the decontamination cradle in May 2001. Previous page bottom: Both X-45A's outside the hanger at Edwards AFB. Above: AV-1 undergoing ground wiring testing at Edwards. Right: A technician works on AV-1 during final assembly. DARPA

The first of 2 X-45A's, AV-1, was completed in September 2000 and Boeing rolled the vehicle out at St Louis, Missouri on the 27th of the month. It was clear that the X-45 could trace its design lineage back to the X-36, with much of the technology developed for the X-36 program feeding into the X-45 program. Another program, which showed clear design lineage leading to the X-45, was the Boeing Bird of Pray technology demonstrator, which made its first flight in 1996.

AV-1 was delivered to the NASA DFRC at Edwards AFB on-board a USAF Boeing C-17A Globmaster III strategic transport aircraft on 8 November 2000. The second X-45, AV-2, was delivered to Dryden by a USAF Lockheed Martin C-5 Galaxy transport aircraft on 15 May 2001.

The X-45A GVT (Ground Vibration Test) was conducted on AV-1 in January 2001 and weapons loading demonstrations were conducted on the vehicle on 21 May that year. The first low speed taxi trials were conducted on 26 September 2001 with further taxi tests conducted on 24 October. The first high-speed taxi tests were conducted on 20 April 2002 in preparation for the first flight.

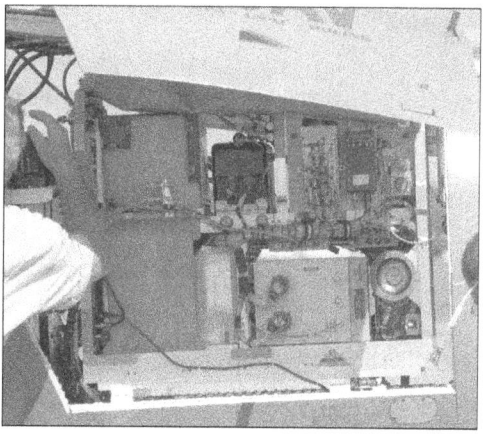

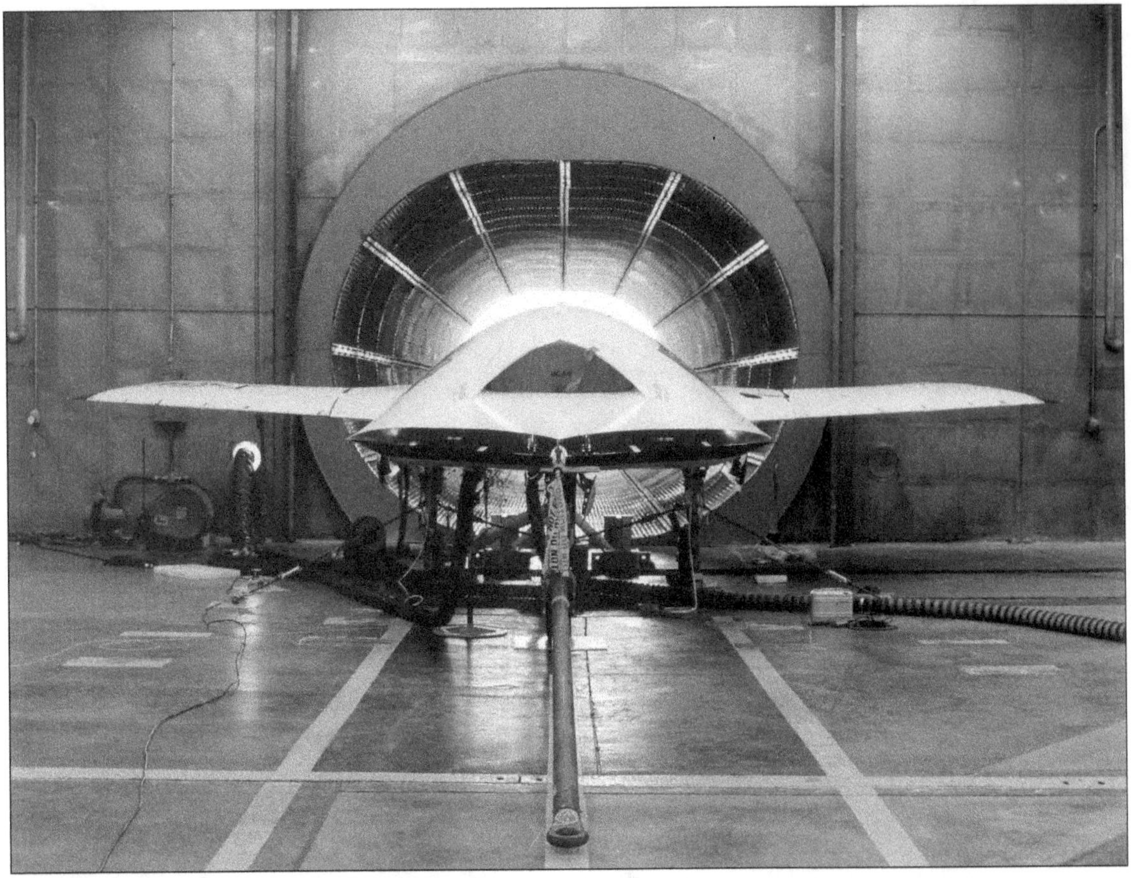

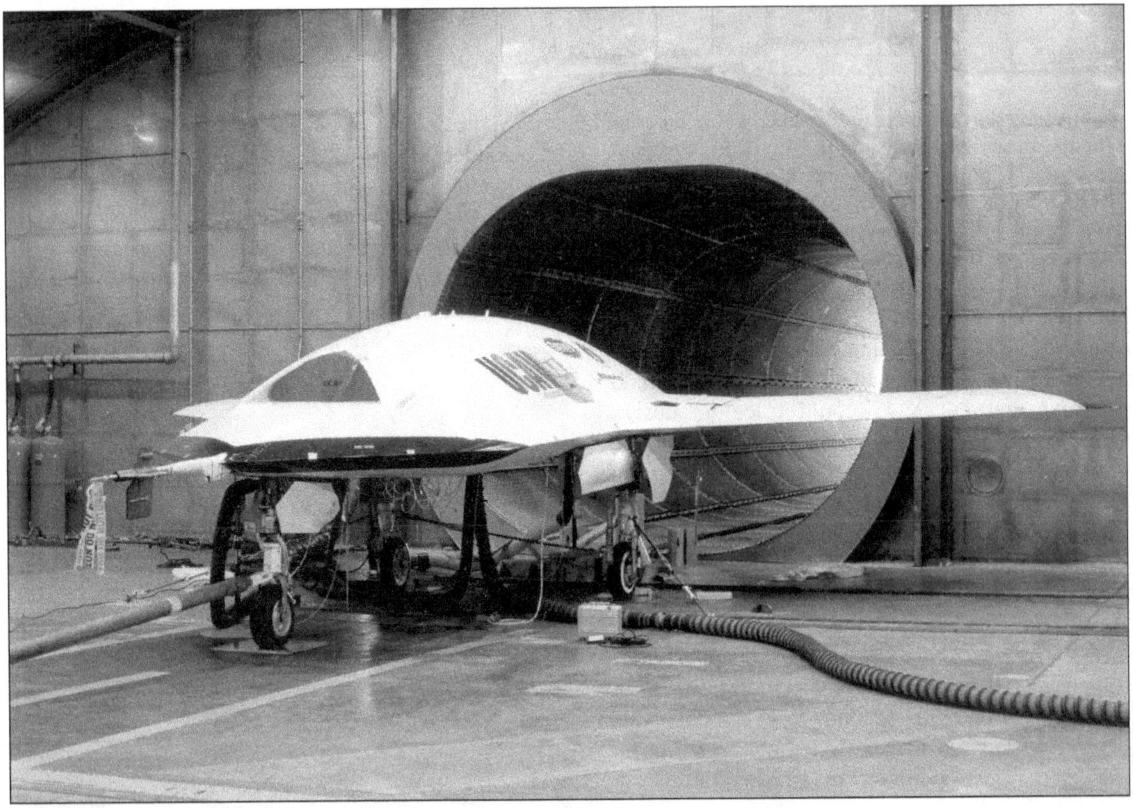

Previous page and this page: The X-45A undergoes engine testing prior to embarking upon taxi trials leading to the first flight. A single Honeywell F124-GA-100 non-afterburning turbofan engine powers the X-45A vehicles. DARPA

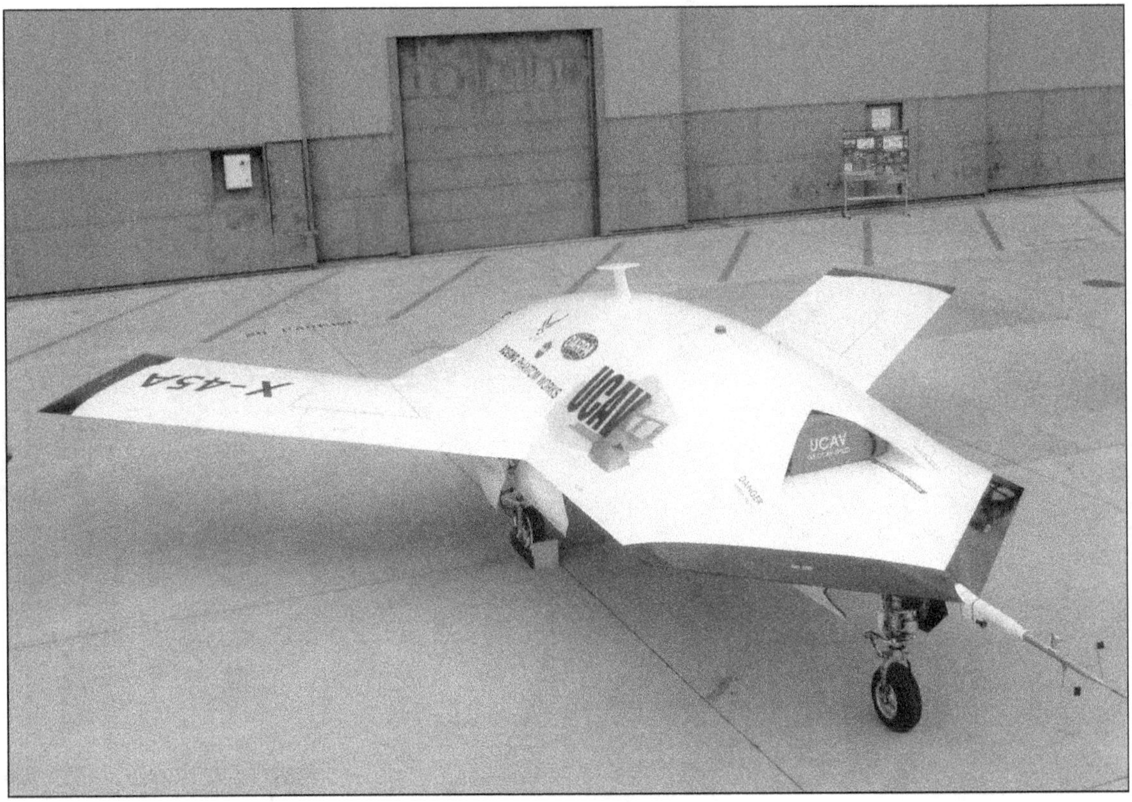
X-45A
UCAV
UCAV

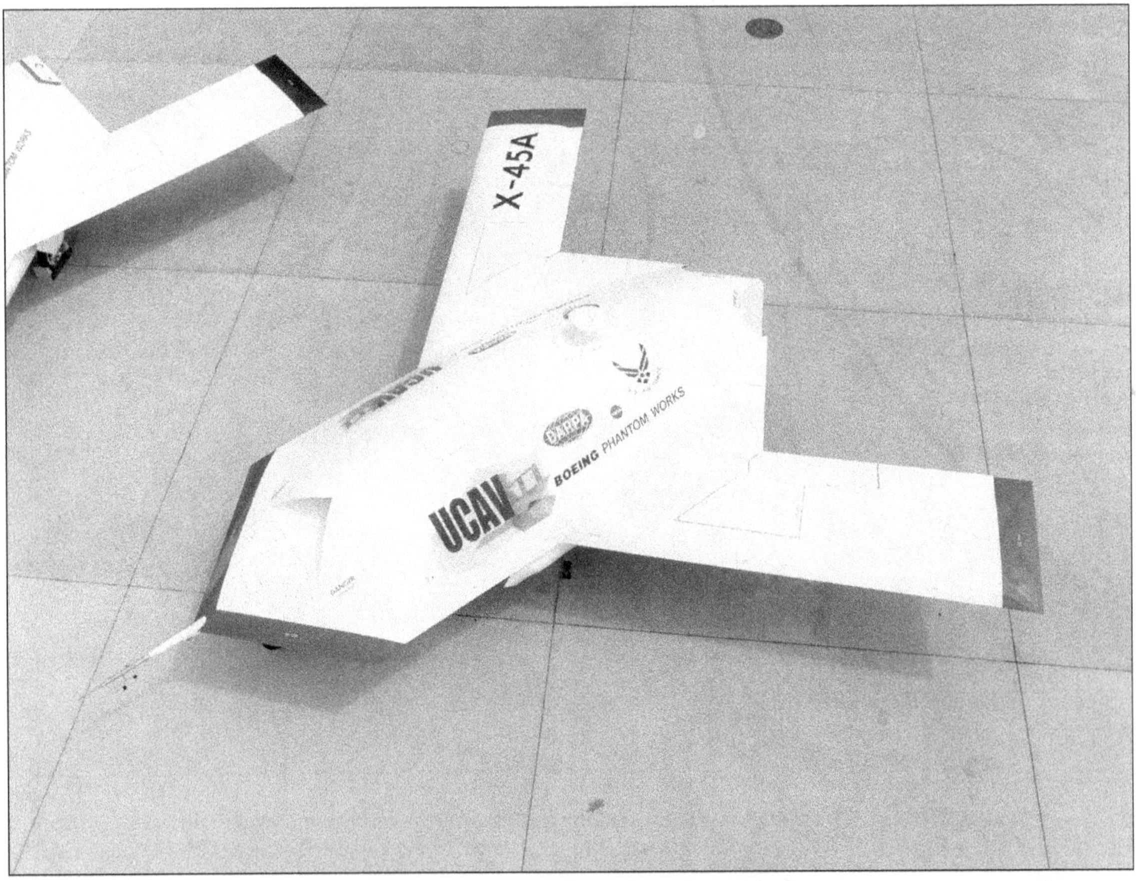
X-45A
DARPA
BOEING PHANTOM WORKS
UCAV

Previous page top: X-45A, AV-1 sits outside a hanger at an Edwards AFB media day. Previous page bottom: AV-2 sits on the ramp at Edwards. Above: The two X-45A vehicles and the Lockheed T-33 UCAV surrogate are displayed at Edwards AFB during the media day. AV-1 is nearest the T-33 with AV-2 on the outside. All DARPA **Right: Both X-45A's parked together at Edwards AFB. AV-1 is at the left with AV-2 to the right.** DARPA

The maiden flight of the first X-45A was originally scheduled for early 2001, but was delayed, eventually taking place on 22 May 2002, beginning the flight-testing of four progressively more capable software blocks. The aircraft took-off from Edwards, AFB, California at 07:26 am and flew for 14 minutes, attaining an airspeed of 195-knots (360-km/h) and an altitude of 7,500-ft. During the flight, vehicle flight characteristics and basic aircraft operations including the command and control link between the X-45A and the ground-based mission control station were demonstrated.

Prior to the first flight of AV-1, the T-33 UCAV surrogate conducted test flights equipped with the X-45A VMC (Vehicle Management Computer), which incorporated the GPS (Global Positioning System) and other systems. This flight was conducted with the T-33 on autopilot, validating the mission plans and assisting with training of ground controllers. The T-33 was used to rehearse X-45A flights, and could act as a UCAV surrogate and fly test missions to assist with the wider J-UCAS program.

On 13 June 2002, AV-1 conducted its second flight, which lasted 32 minutes. Following the second flight AV-1 was grounded for a planned software upgrade with less than 1 hour of flight time under its belt. AV-2 was not allocated any Block 1 test objectives and was instead used to pave the way for the Block 2 test series, but not before AV-1 and AV-2, which had yet to fly were present at an open day at Edwards AFB on 11 July 2002, giving a public face to the program.

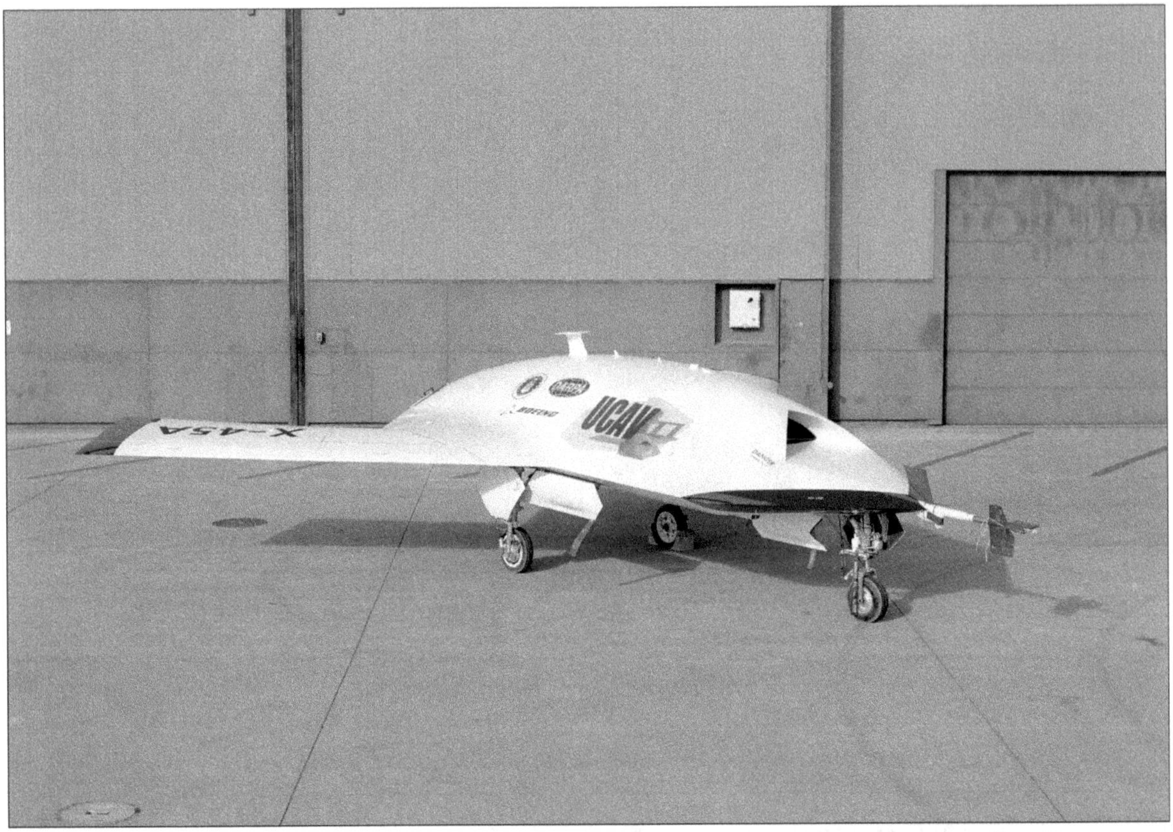
X-45A
UCAV
BOEING

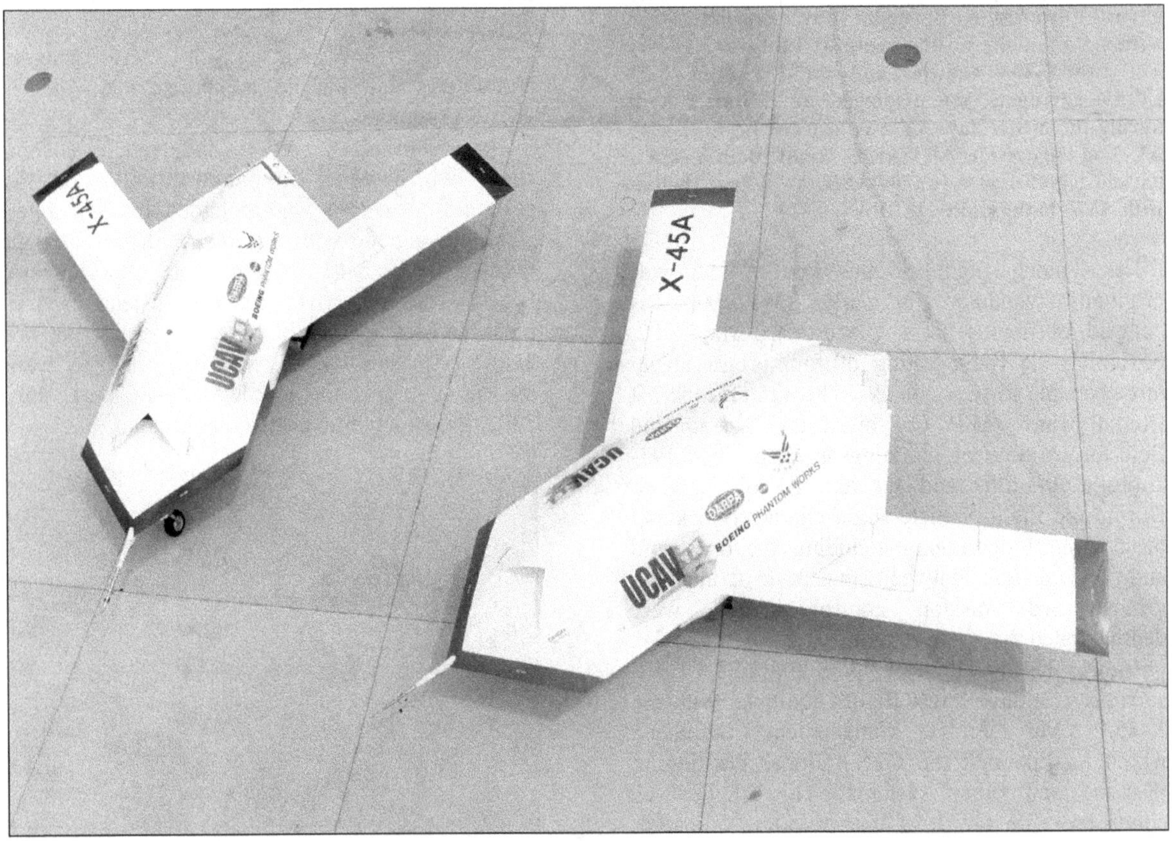
X-45A
UCAV
BOEING PHANTOM WORKS
X-45A
UCAV
DARPA
BOEING PHANTOM WORKS

Previous page top: X-45A AV-2 outside the hanger at Dryden. Previous page bottom: Both X-45A demonstrators are seen together at Edwards AFB. Above: X-45A AV-1 is seen outside the hanger at the DFRC, Edwards AFB. DARPA

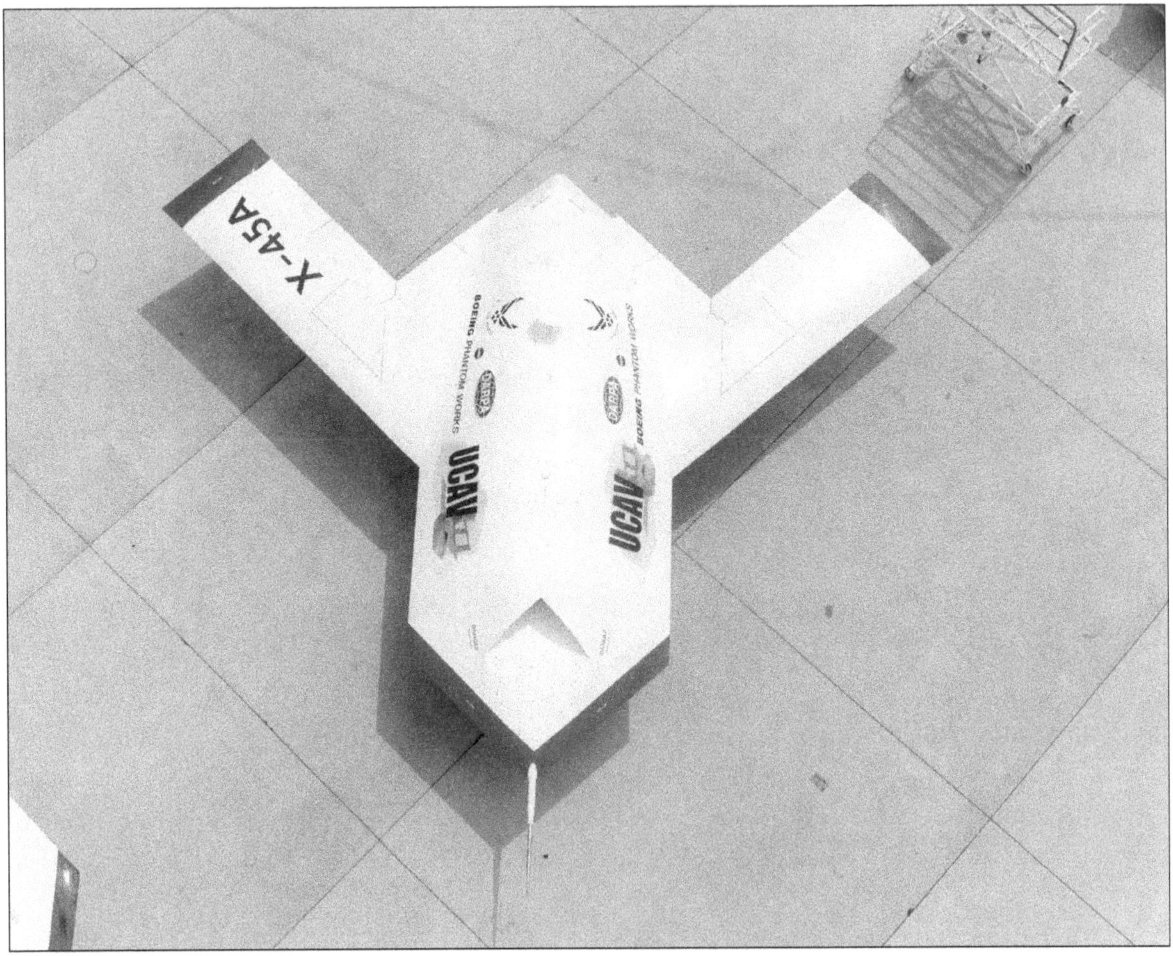

Above: Overhead view of the second X-45A, AV-2, showing to advantage the low-set wing, blended fuselage and the 'W' shaped planform trailing edge. Below: AV-2 (nearest) was displayed at the UCAV media day at Edwards AFB, California along with the first X-45A AV-1 (centre) and other elements of the UCAV system. Right: AV-1 got air under its wheels on its first flight on 22 May 2002. DARPA

AV-2 conducted its maiden flight from Edwards AFB on 21 November 2002; reaching an altitude of 7,500-ft and a speed of 195-kts during the 29-munite flight. By this time AV-1 had completed 5 flights, expanding the flight envelope and completing 60% of the airworthiness test objectives. It was initially planned for the undercarriage to be retracted in flight by AV-1 on its fourth flight, but this was subsequently delayed with AV-1 retracting the undercarriage in flight during its sixth flight, which lasted 40-minutes on 19 December 2002. AV-1 flew at altitudes up to 7,500-ft and an air speed of 195-kts.

UCAV
DARPA
BOEING PHANTOM WORKS

UCAV
DARPA
BOEING PHANTOM WORKS

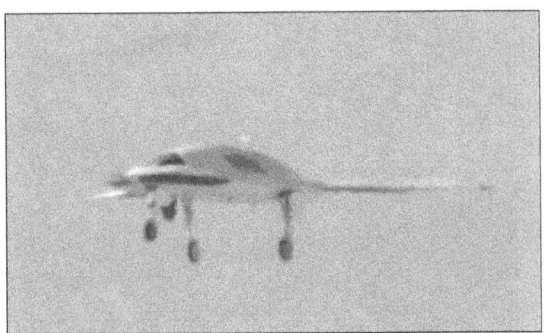

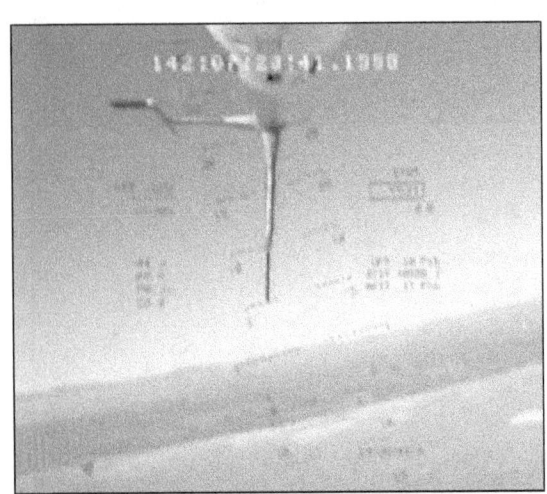

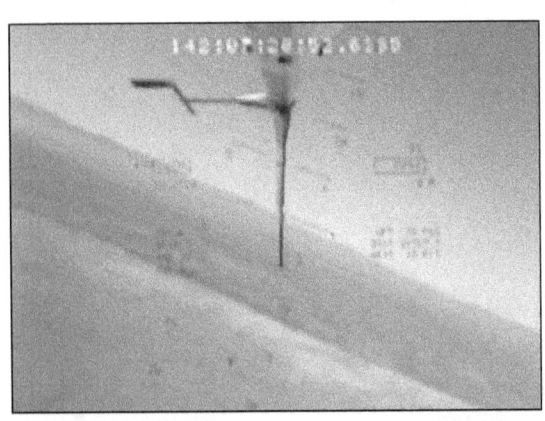

AV-1 during initial climb to final approach on its maiden flight: Top left and centre top left: right turn on initial climb. Centre bottom left: HUD (Heads-Up Display) initial climb. Bottom left: HUD left turn on initial climb. Top right and centre top right: Initial climb. Centre bottom right: Final approach. Bottom right: HUD view on final approach. DARPA

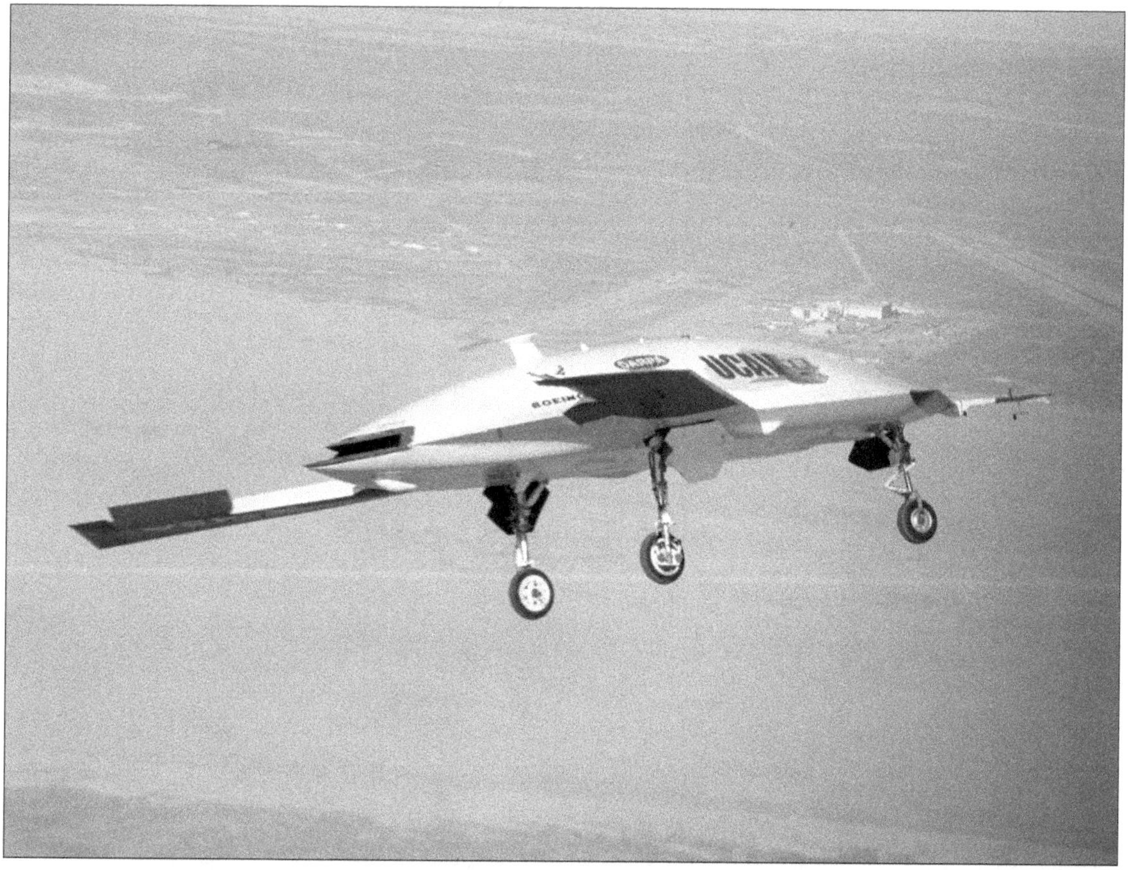
UCAV
BOEING

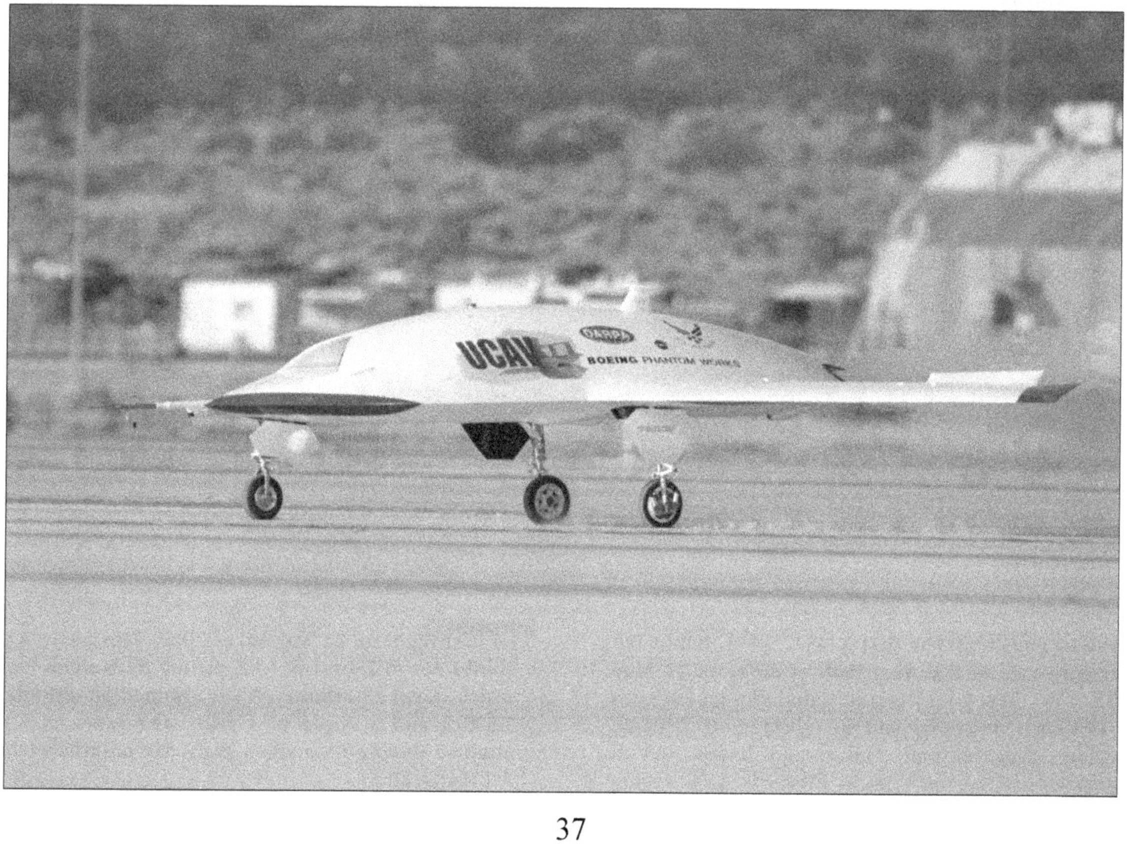
UCAV
BOEING PHANTOM WORKS

Previous page top: The first X-45A, AV-1, banks left over Edwards AFB during its first flight on 22 May 2002. AV-1 flew for 14 minutes attaining an airspeed of 195-kts (360-km/h) and an altitude of 7,500-ft. Previous page bottom: The second X-45A, AV-2, commences its take-off run at Edwards AFB during its first flight on 21 November 2002. This page: AV-2 climbs out of Edwards AFB during its maiden flight, which lasted 29-minutes. AV-2 attained an altitude of 7,500-ft and a speed of 195-kts, the same as AV-1 attained during its maiden flight six months earlier. All NASA DFRC

AV-1 during its first flight on 22 May 2002. The undercarriage remained extended for the first 5 flights of the program. NASA DFRC

Prior to the maiden flight of AV-2, further progress was made in the ground-based segment of the development program. In October 2002, a distributed multi-vehicle control capability for the mission control segment of the UCAV system was successfully demonstrated at the Boeing SIL (Simulation Integration Laboratory) at its Seattle facility. The Build 2.0 mission control software was the first release of the extensive Block 2 capability designed to allow multi-vehicle control, dynamic mission planning and satellite communications capability. The build 2 release was designed to allow a single pilot operator on the ground to control two X-45A's in the air at once. In preparation for the multi-vehicle flights in 2003, the new software was further enhanced and then integrated with the X-45A air vehicles.

On 28 February 2003, the X-45A team successfully completed the Block 1 demonstration phase, during which 48 'discrete' flights, laboratory and simulation demonstrations were conducted, which reduced the risks associated with new technologies and systems of the UCAV program covering the air vehicle, integration, mission control and supportability. During this phase the two X-45A demonstrators conducted 16 flights during almost 13 flight-hours since AV-1 conducted its first flight in May 2002. The Block 1 demonstrations culminated in two flights (including the last block 1 flight on 28 February) that verified the safe operation of the weapons bay doors at speeds up to Mach 0.75 and altitudes of 35,000-ft, which was the maximum planned altitude and speed for the X-45A.

One of the X-45A demonstrator vehicles lands back at Edwards AFB following a test flight over the vast range complexes adjacent to the Edwards complex. DARPA

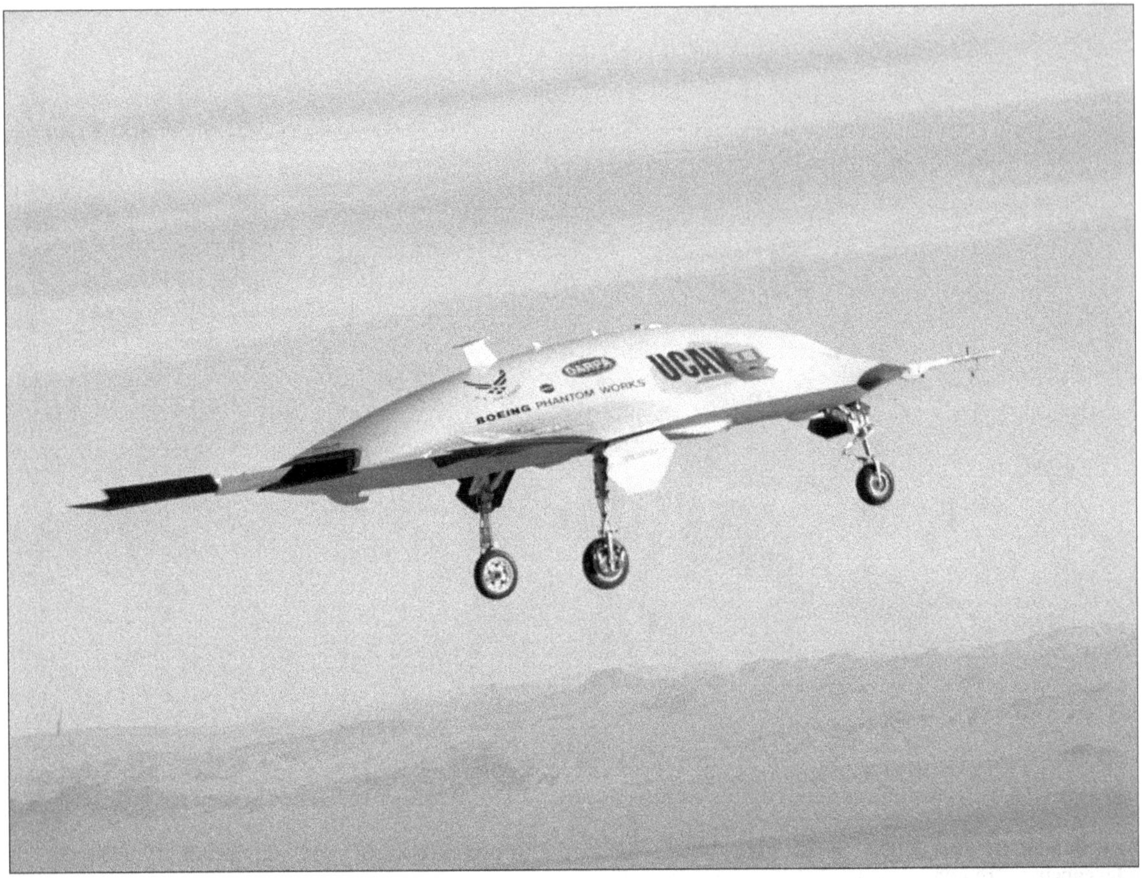
UCAV
BOEING PHANTOM WORKS

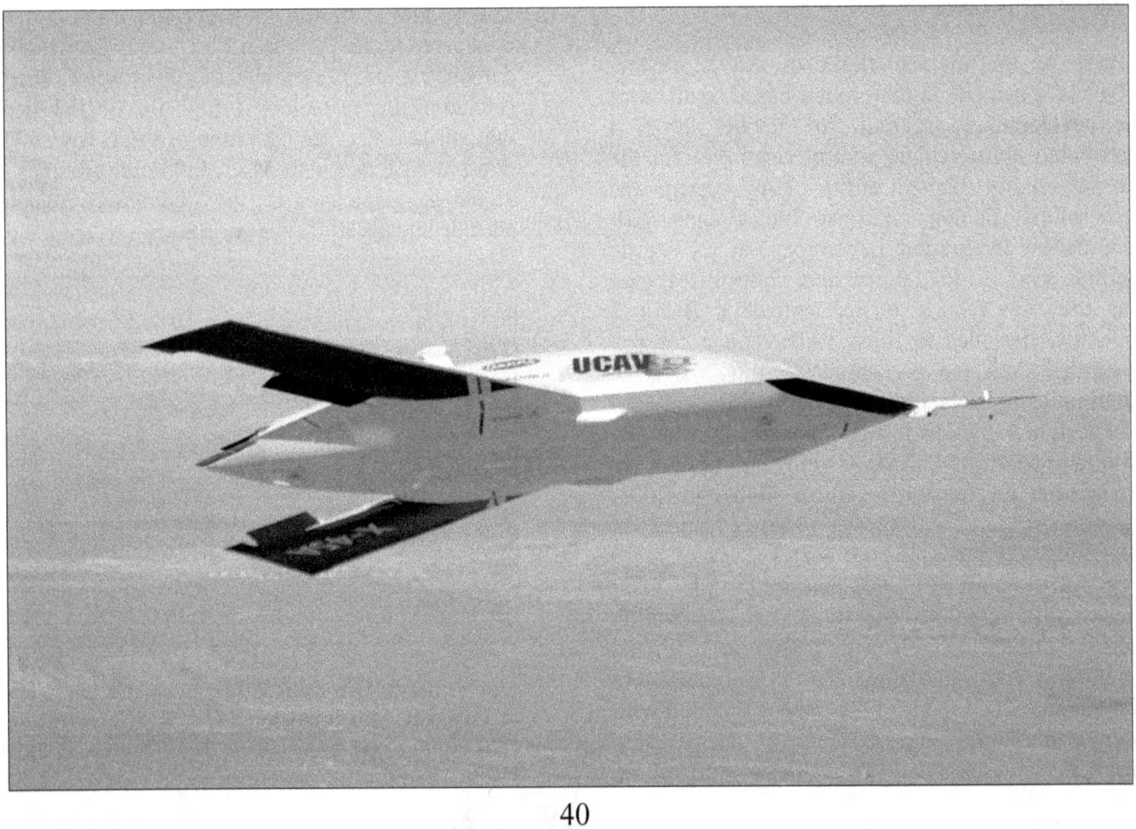
UCAV

Previous page top: With the first flight of AV-2 on 21 November 2002, the program moved into the Block 2 software flight-testing. **Previous page bottom:** X-45A AV-1 is seen over the desert near Edwards during its sixth flight on 19 December 2002. **This page:** During the sixth flight of AV-1 on 19 December 2002, the X-45A's undercarriage was retracted in flight for the first time. This milestone had initially been planned for the fourth flight. NASA DFRC **Right:** This murky poor quality still shows AV-1 in a gentle starboard turn with flaps deployed. DARPA

Key Block 1 demonstrations included:

• **Wing Attachment:** The team demonstrated X-45A wing removal from the transport container, wing handling, wing attachment, and the process for verification and inspection.
• **Autonomous Taxi:** The X-45A demonstrated autonomous taxi with the ability of the operator to intervene in the event of an emergency. It also demonstrated accurate ground navigation and waypoint steering, air vehicle position control, and reliable communication links.
• **Concept of Operations Simulations:** Boeing's UCAV System Integration Laboratory in Seattle, demonstrated several advanced attributes of the MCS (Mission Control Segment) in support of potential UCAV concept of operations. The Lab also demonstrated decision aiding software and multiple levels of autonomy in the MCS, as well as several approaches to vehicle hand-off between two different operators. Simulations also demonstrated decision aiding related to target engagement.

Top: With the first flight of the second X-45A, AV-2, Boeing, DARPA and the USAF stepped the program up a gear, being able to conduct more ground and flight-testing than was the case with only a single vehicle. **Above:** X-45A AV-1 is seen with its undercarriage retracted during its sixth flight on 19 December 2002. This flight lasted 40 minutes and AV-1 was flown at speeds up to 195-kts. NASA DFRC

The addition of AV-2, here chocked on the ramp at Edwards, allowed testing to be conducted at a higher tempo than would have been the case with a single vehicle. Right: Checks are conducted on AV-1 before a flight from Edwards. DARPA

- **Distributed Control:** During flight tests, the team demonstrated the distributed control capability of the UCAV system, passing control between the Mission Control Shelter and the Mission Control Van and back again.
- **Loss of Communication Response:** The UCAV system demonstrated the ability to autonomously respond to a complete loss of communication with the UCAV ground station by executing the appropriate onboard contingency management plan. As planned, the air vehicle returned to base and landed safely upon loss of communication.
- **Four-Dimensional Navigation:** Four-dimensional navigation is the ability to accurately control time as well as position. The X-45A was given Time of Arrival (TOA) commands so the vehicle would reach a certain waypoints (defined by latitude, longitude, and altitude) in the mission plan at specified times. The X-45A automatically adjusted its speed to overcome headwinds and changed its flight plan to arrive at the specified waypoints at the times commanded by the operator. Four-dimensional navigation is intended for coordinating attacks in support of combat missions and is the foundation for the UCAV's multi-ship coordinated flight capability, where UCAV's will use this capability to arrive simultaneously at a designated waypoint and autonomously form up into a coordinated flight package, thereby greatly reducing the operator's workload.

By late March 2003, the X-45A team had conducted demonstrations proving an autonomous UCAV controlled from a ground station could be integrated into air traffic controlled airspace along with inhabited aircraft. The demonstration began in

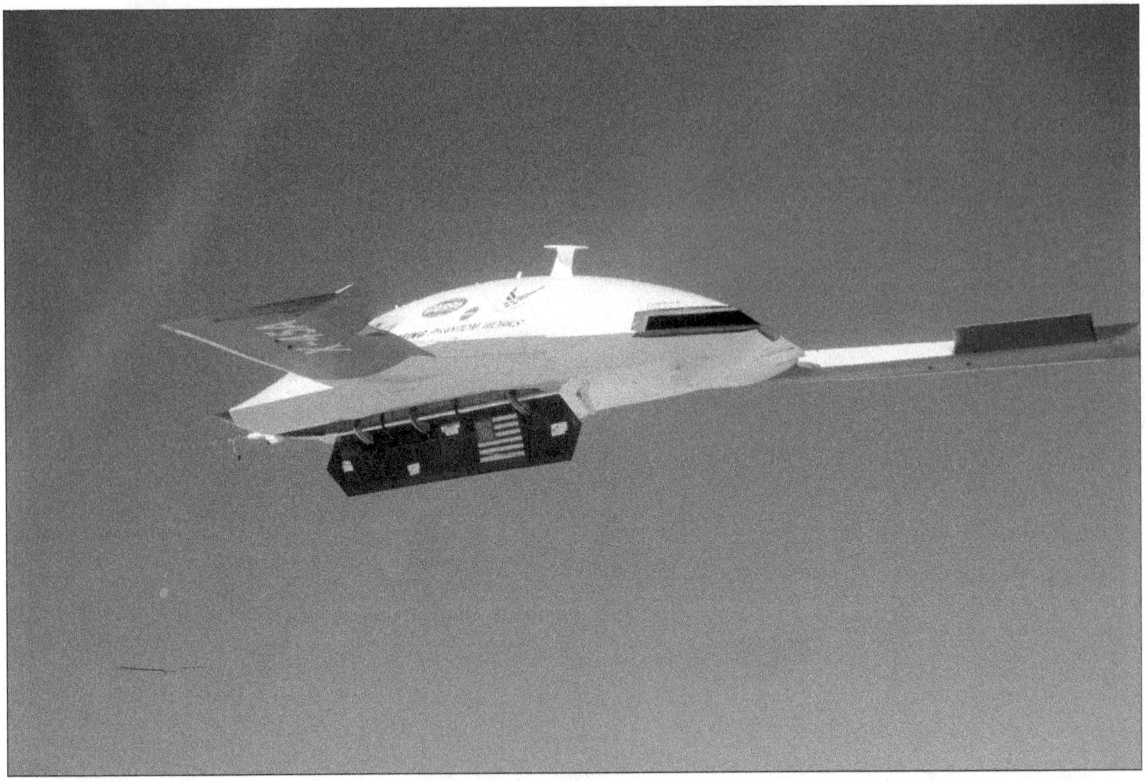

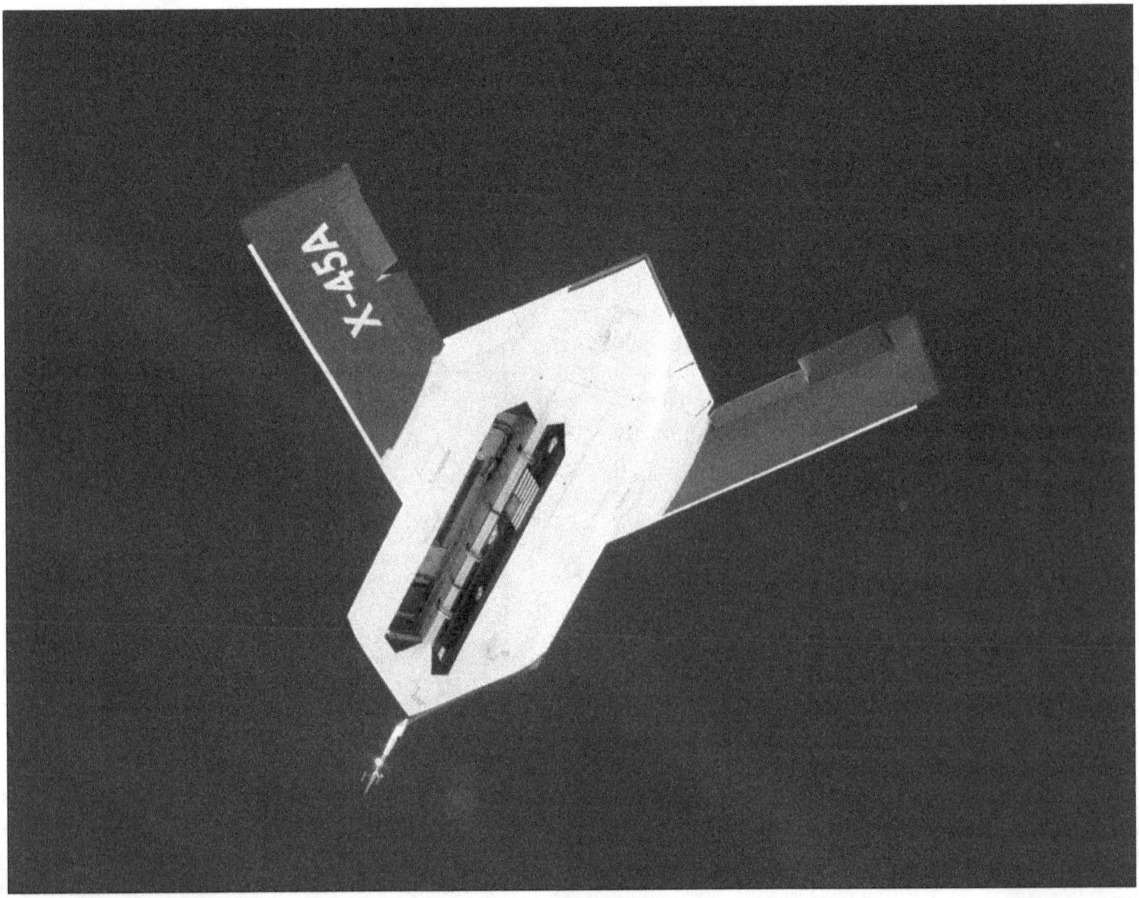
X-45A

Previous page top and bottom: AV-1 conducted its 13th flight on 21 February 2003. During this flight the vehicle opened its portside weapons bay door in flight. NASA DFRC **This page above: This view of the X-45A from the side-on aspect shows the serrated edges on the weapons bay doors designed to increase the 'stealth' qualities of the UCAV.** DARPA

February 2003, with the initial phase consisting of five flights, which conducted from Dryden, during which airspace procedures and basic functionality in a low tempo of operations environment were conducted. During this phase the Lockheed T-33 UCAV surrogate was flown into and out of controlled airspace several times during each flight, during which the aircraft integrated with other air traffic in the base pattern. A further eight flights were conducted in March from Eglin AFB to test the system in a high tempo operational environment.

This test series, which was the first of the Block 2 UCAV demonstrations, did not use any of the X-45A vehicles, but utilised the T-33 surrogate equipped with an avionics package that was fully representative of the X-45A. The T-33 surrogate UCAV could autonomously fly pre-planned missions. The flights had a test pilot aboard; however, this was "hands-off", although the pilot could take control in an emergency if required. The flights also provided training for pilot controllers on the ground as the T-33 could be controlled from the ground in the same way as the X-45A.

The X-45A program was aimed only at demonstrating a viable UCAV concept for land-based operations with the USAF. Therefore, the undercarriage system did not require to be designed for the stresses associated with aircraft carrier operations. DARPA

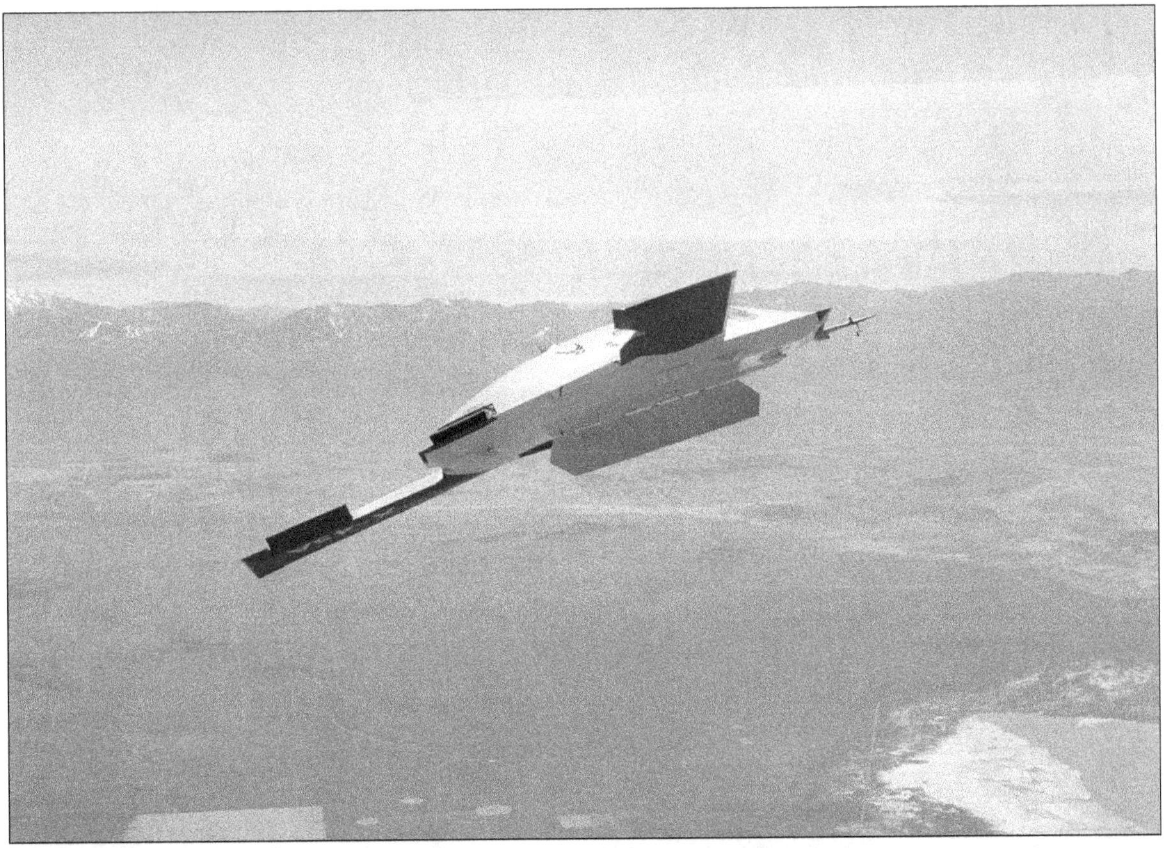

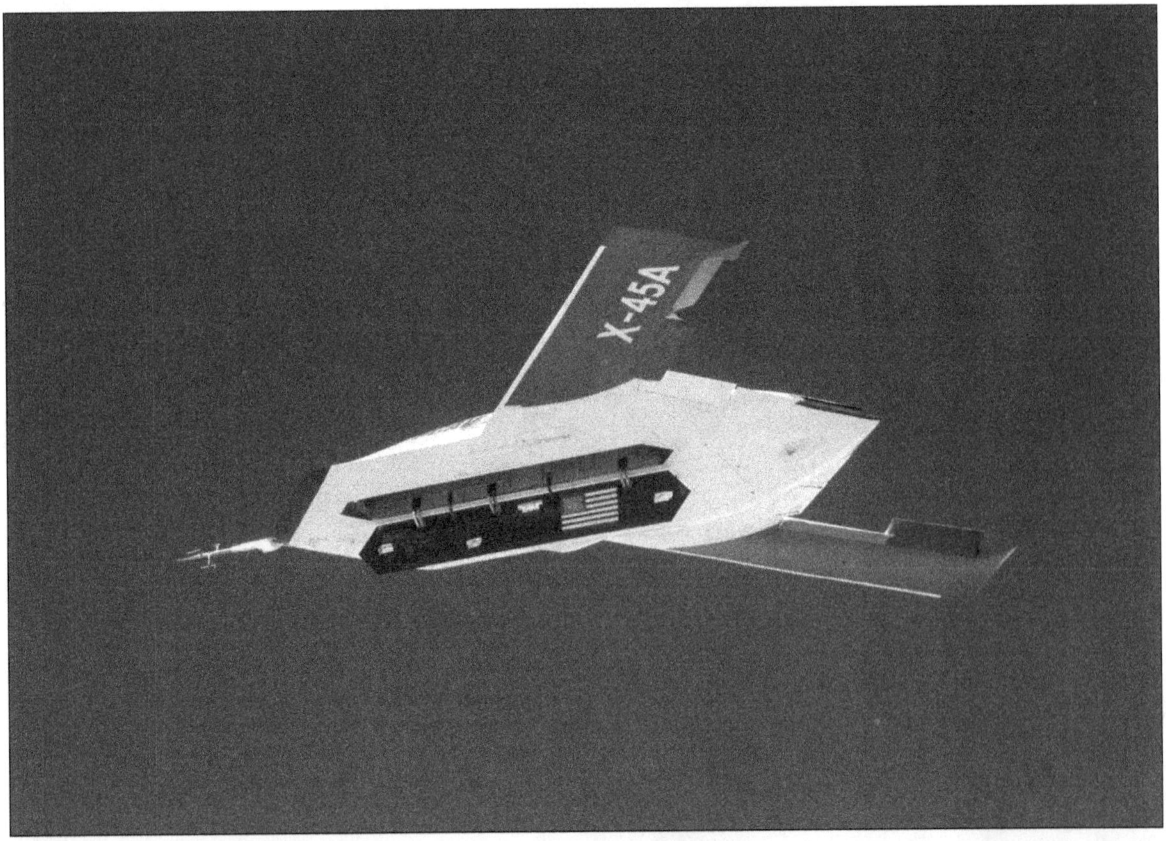
X-45A

Previous page: The weapons bays on the X-45A vehicles ran almost the entire length of the fuselage as can be seen in this view of AV-1 on its 13th flight. The X-45A was designed to carry a 1,500-lb payload, with the new generation of small smart munitions being the favoured choice. **Above:** From the side-on aspect the X-45A presents a very small visual signature courtesy of its small size and tailless configuration. NASA DFRC **Right:** The Lockheed T-33 UCAV surrogate flies along the US coastline. DARPA

During the flights, controllers on the ground communicated with air traffic controllers to change the T-33's flight profile when required for separation from other air traffic, holding, and during simulated missed approaches. This flight phase enabled the program to amass experience in flying a UCAV (in this case the T-33 UCAV surrogate) vehicle in a busy air traffic environment. This test phase also saw the first use of a Link 16 anti-jam, secure communications data link, which was used to remotely operate the T-33 from the ground control station. By early March 2003, seven of the 40 planned Block 2 demonstrations had been conducted.

While the T-33 was used to kick start Block 2 flight-testing, the X-45A vehicles completed the Block 1 testing, during which 16 test flights were conducted by the X-45A air vehicles. Block 1 testing consisted of 48 laboratory, simulation and flight tests, which were mainly focused on initial systems checkout.

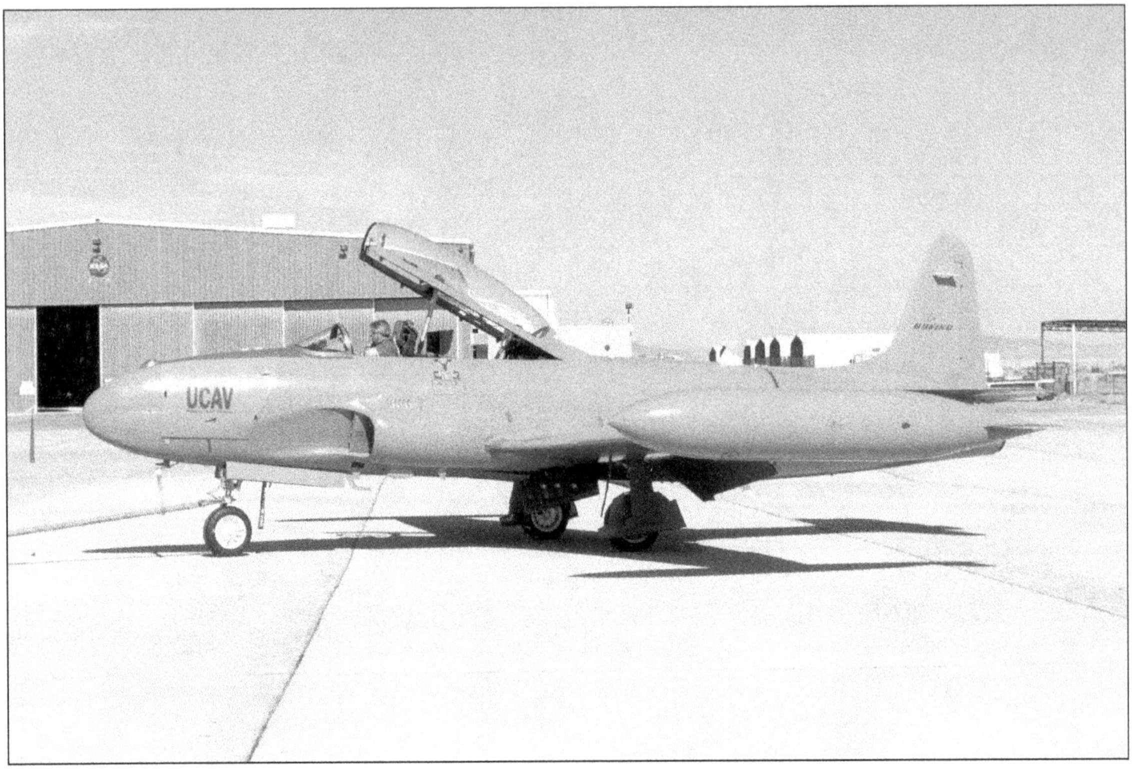
UCAV

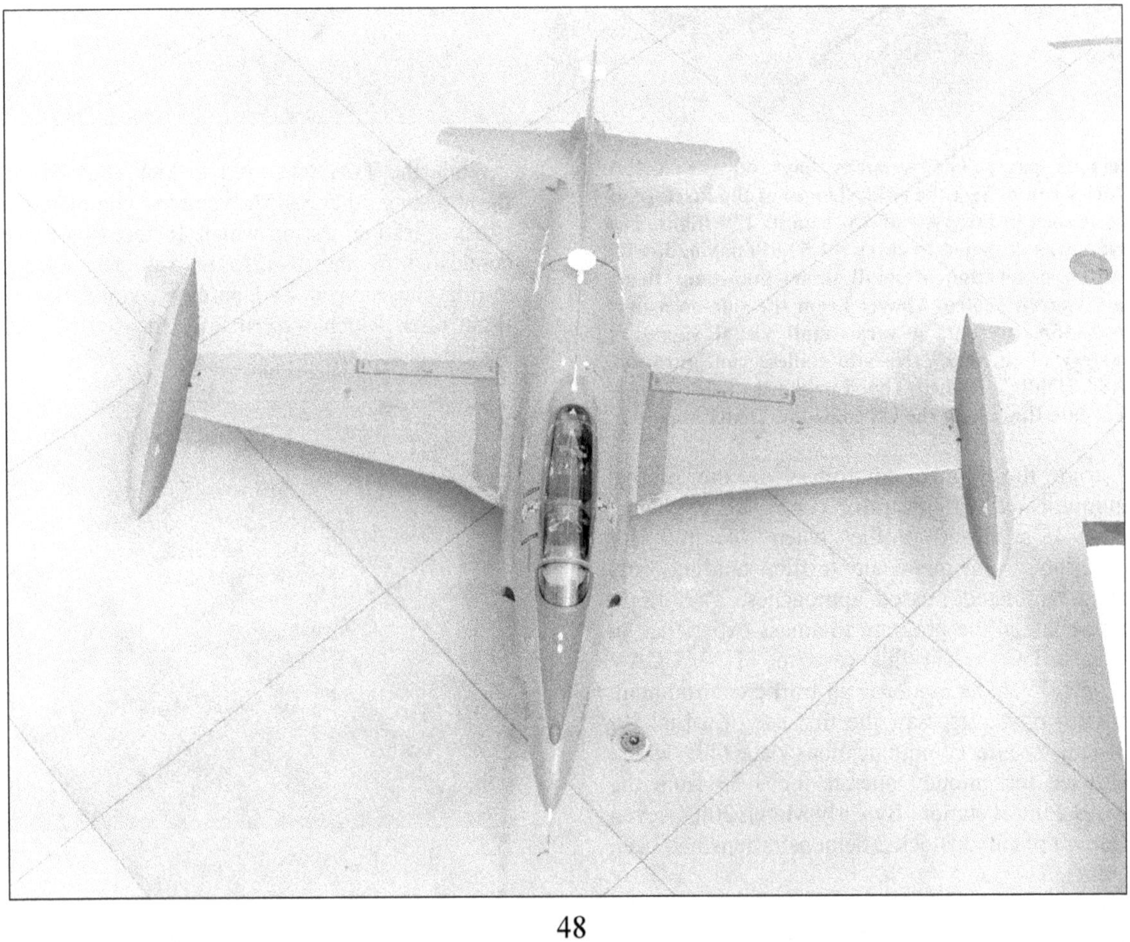

Previous page: The T-33 UCAV Surrogate could autonomously fly pre-planned missions. Although a pilot was carried, the missions were flown "hands-off" although the pilot could take control in an emergency. The T-33 was an ideal choice as a UCAV surrogate as it was of similar size to an X-45A. This page: In early 2003 a block 2 demonstration saw the Lockheed T-33 UCAV surrogate flown into and out of controlled airspace several times during each flight, during which the aircraft integrated with other air traffic in the base pattern. These demonstrations did not use any of the X-45A vehicles, but utilised the T-33 surrogate equipped with an avionics package, which was fully representative of the X-45A. DARPA

Block 2 testing continued throughout 2003 and on 4 November that year the X-45A program commenced a series of flight-tests designed to demonstrate the two X-45A vehicles ability to fly co-ordinated operations together. During this series of test-flights the X-45A's demonstrated communication links for air to air and air to ground co-ordination leading to the release of inert small smart bombs from one of the vehicles. The communication link would see an X-45A controlled from another location beyond line-of-sight other than Edwards AFB. In this phase around 30-35 X-45A sorties were planned supported by an additional 12 or so sorties by the T-33 UCAV surrogate.

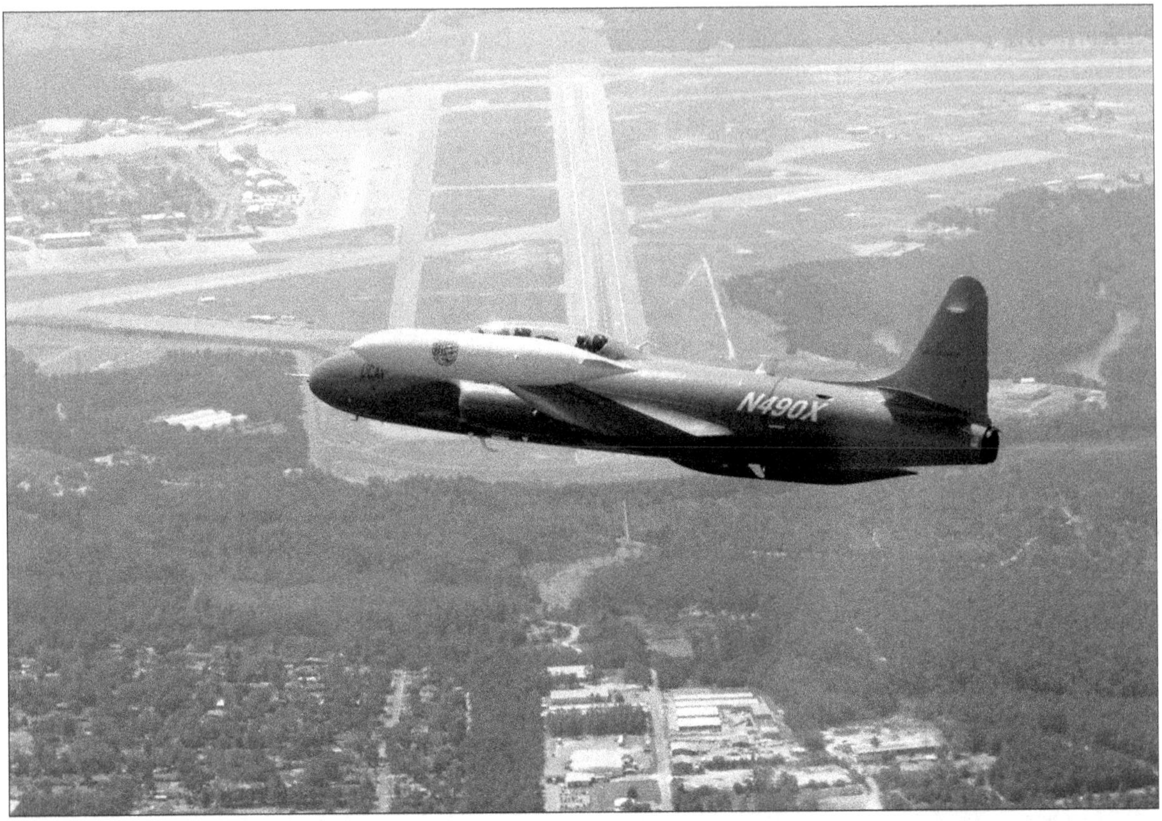
N490X

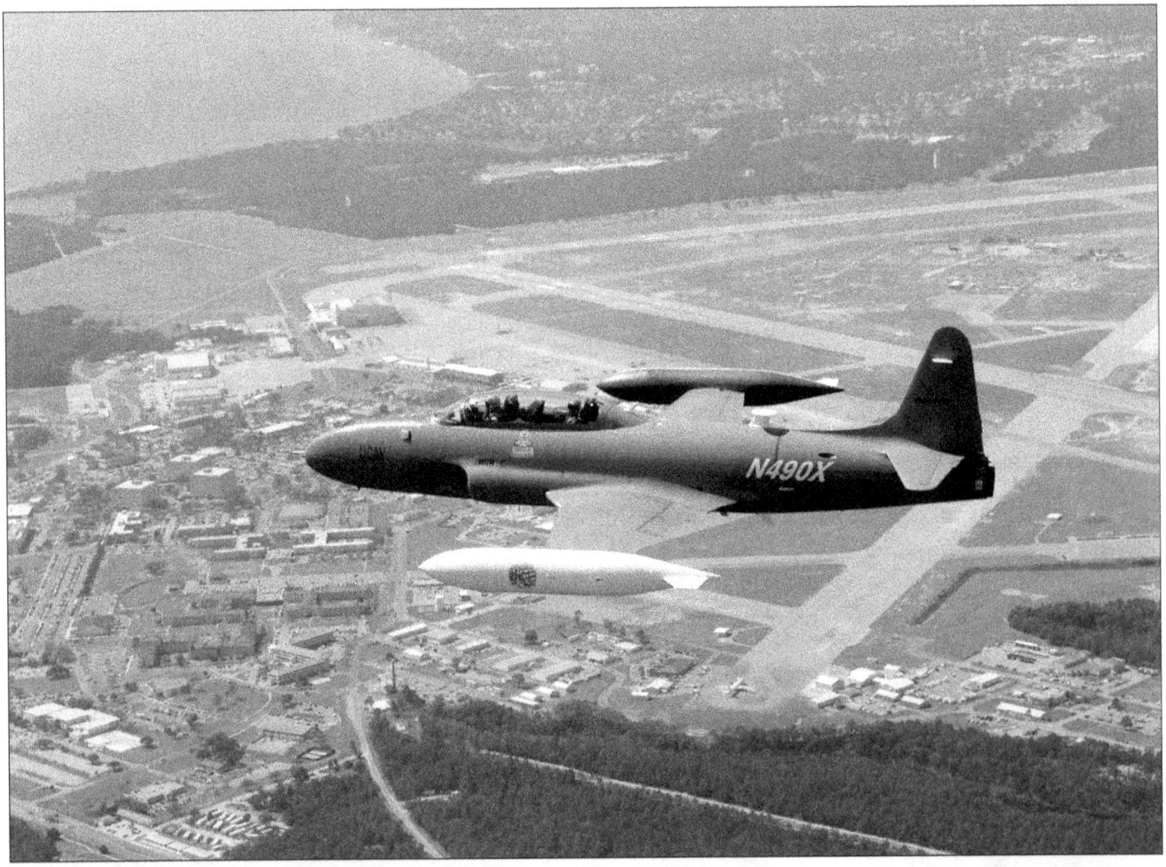
N490X

Previous page and this page: For the Block 2 test series the T-33 UCAV surrogate operated from Eglin AFB, Florida. DARPA **The T-33 could be used for a number of tests in support of the X-45A program.** DARPA

Block 2 X-45 vehicle flight-testing began with a number of checkout flights involving a single X-45A before commencing to co-ordinated flights involving an X-45A and the T-33 UCAV surrogate and then onto flights involving both X-45A vehicles. Prior to two-ship flights, the X-45A's conducted two-ship coordinated taxi tests.

On 20 March 2004, the X-45A conducted an airborne release of an inert weapon – a small smart bomb. This was the first weapon release from an internal weapon bay of the X-45A. The flight also demonstrated the X-45A's maximum flight envelope with a speed of around 495-mph and an altitude of around 35,000-ft. Proper operation of the weapon bay doors was also verified as was the ability to transmit a radar image to a ground station operator without time and bandwidth constraints.

Prior to this flight, 3 flights were conducted on 11, 13 and 17 March. The 11 March flight was the first of two regression flights to validate software changes. During this flight the X-45A had to be unexpectedly re-directed around the flight pattern when another aircraft declared an in-flight emergency. This unscheduled re-direction showed to a small degree the X-45A's ability to fly in airspace shared by inhabited aircraft. The second regression flight also validated software changes. During these Block 2 software validation flights the X-45A was flown to maximum envelope altitude of 35,000-ft and maximum speed of Mach 0.75. The weapons bay doors were opened and

52

Previous page top: AV-1 is refuelled at Edwards on 21 March 2004. Previous page bottom: AV-1 receives system checks before a test flight in March 2004. DARPA **This page: The NASA DFRC Boeing F/A-18 Hornet #846 flies chase for the X-45A at the start of the weapons drop test conducted on 18 April 2004.** NASA DFRC

Prior to the 18 April 2004 GPS weapon demonstration, an X-45A had released an inert weapon on 20 March. This flight was preceded by three flights conducted in the days before the airborne release, including two regression flights to validate software changes and another flight, which served as a dry run for the 20 March weapon release. NASA DFRC

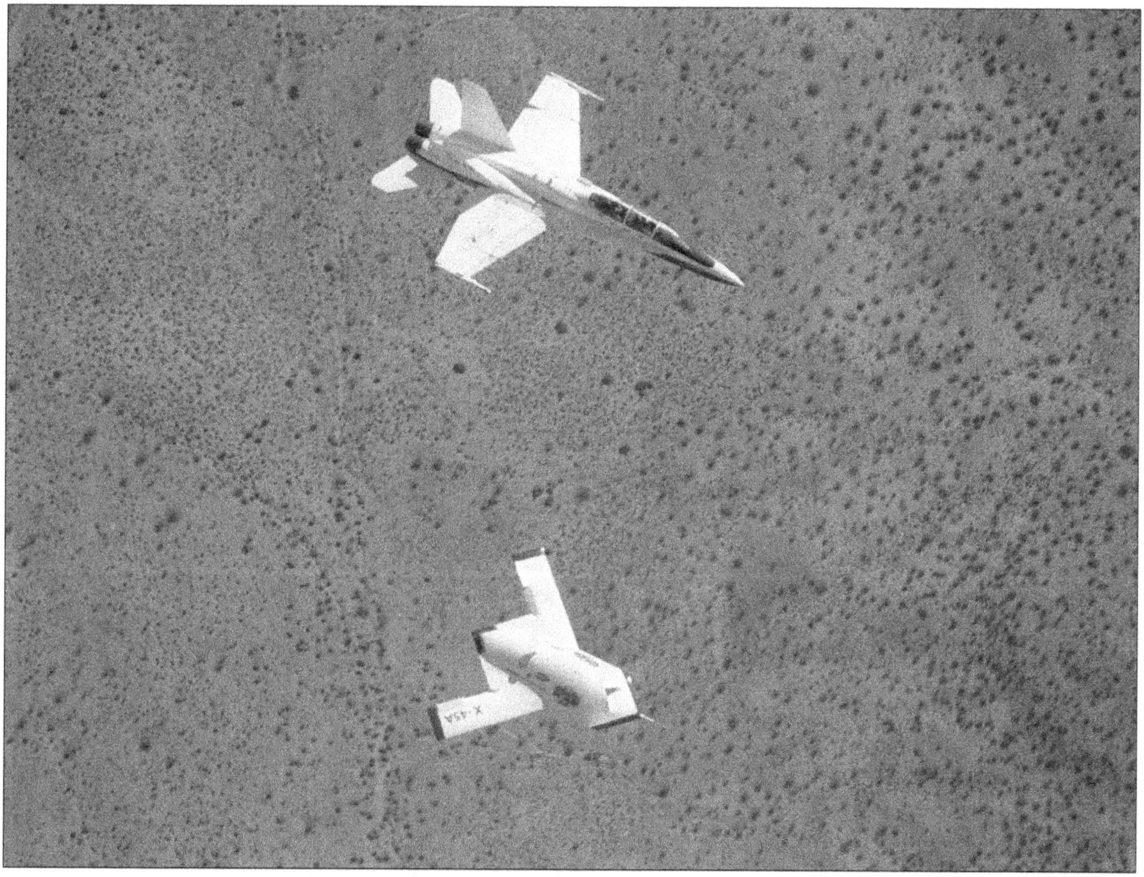
X-45A

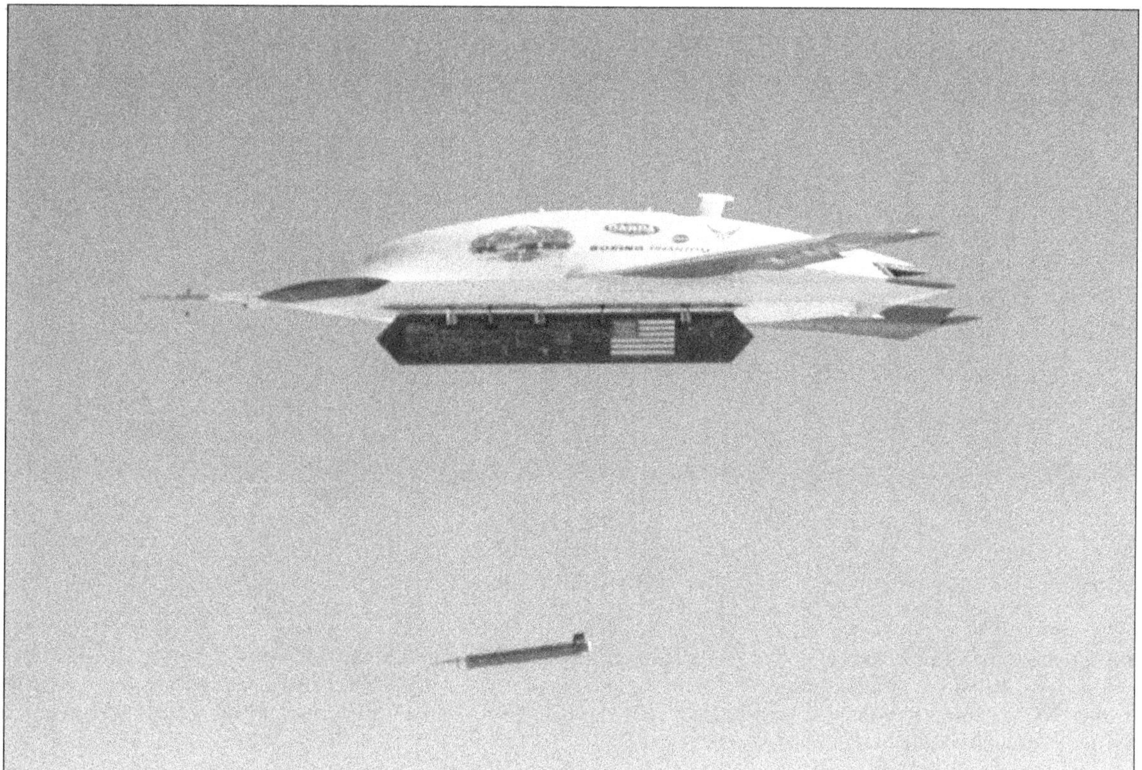

Previous page top: The X-45A flies over the southern Californian desert in along with DFRC Boeing F/A-18 Hornet #846 during the 18 April 2004 weapon demonstration flight. NASA DFRC Previous page bottom and this page: During this demonstration an inert 250-lb class GPS guided bomb released from an internal weapons bay of an X-45A achieved a direct hit on the ground target. DARPA

The three critical commands for weapon release were Target Confirmation, Arm, and Release consent. Once the ground based pilot operator had authorised release of the weapon and once the X-45A UCAV confirmed that it was within range of the target, the GPS-guided weapon was released from the internal weapons bay while flying at an altitude of 35,000-ft and a speed of Mach 0.67 (around 442 mph). An operational weapon released at a similar altitude and speed would have a standoff range of several tens of kilometres. DARPA

58

release over the Naval Air Warfare Centre-Weapons Division China Lake range on 18 April 2004. During this mission an inert 250-lb class GPS guided SDB (Small Diameter Bomb) was released from an internal weapons bay of an X-45A achieving a direct hit on the ground target.

The three critical commands for the weapon release were Target Confirmation, Arm, and Release consent. Once the operator had authorised release of the weapon and the X-45A confirmed that it was within range of the target, the SDB was released at an altitude of 35,000-ft and a speed of Mach 0.67. The X-45A autonomously conducted all required manoeuvres, operation of the weapon bay doors and the actual release of the weapon while under supervision of the ground based operator.

Above and below: Video still showing the inert 250-lb GPS-guided weapon about to impact the target and on impact. The target for the test was a derelict military vehicle on the test range. Right: An F/A-18 Hornet flies slow chase as an X-45A land at Edwards AFB following an early test flight. DARPA

closed in-flight in preparation for the forthcoming weapon release flights. The flights also demonstrated the ability of the X-45A to transmit a "stored" SAR (Synthetic Aperture Radar) image to the ground station within bandwidth and timeline constraints.

During the 17 March flight the X-45A completed a captive carry of the GPS guided small smart bomb as well as validating the new software. The same mission planning used for the 17 March captive carry flight was also used for the 20 March weapon release flight in order to 'dry run' weapon release procedures. The successful release of the inert weapon paved the way for a further weapon

On 7 May 2004, an X-45A successfully communicated with a T-33 UCAV surrogate while in-flight. The X-45A exchanged data with the T-33 through a system known as the FDL (Fighter Data Link), which is a secure data link allowing the transfer of electronic data between different platforms. The X-45A was flying at an altitude of 14,000-ft and airspeed of 228 mph. The aircraft manoeuvred around each other ensuring a good communications link was established.

In preparation for the joint flight tests, the 2 X-45A's conducted joint taxi trials on 27 May 2004 with both vehicles moving under their own power under the control of a single pilot operator in preparation for joint coordinated flight testing. The vehicles demonstrated ground turns of up to 90-degrees and turnarounds with speeds reaching 20-

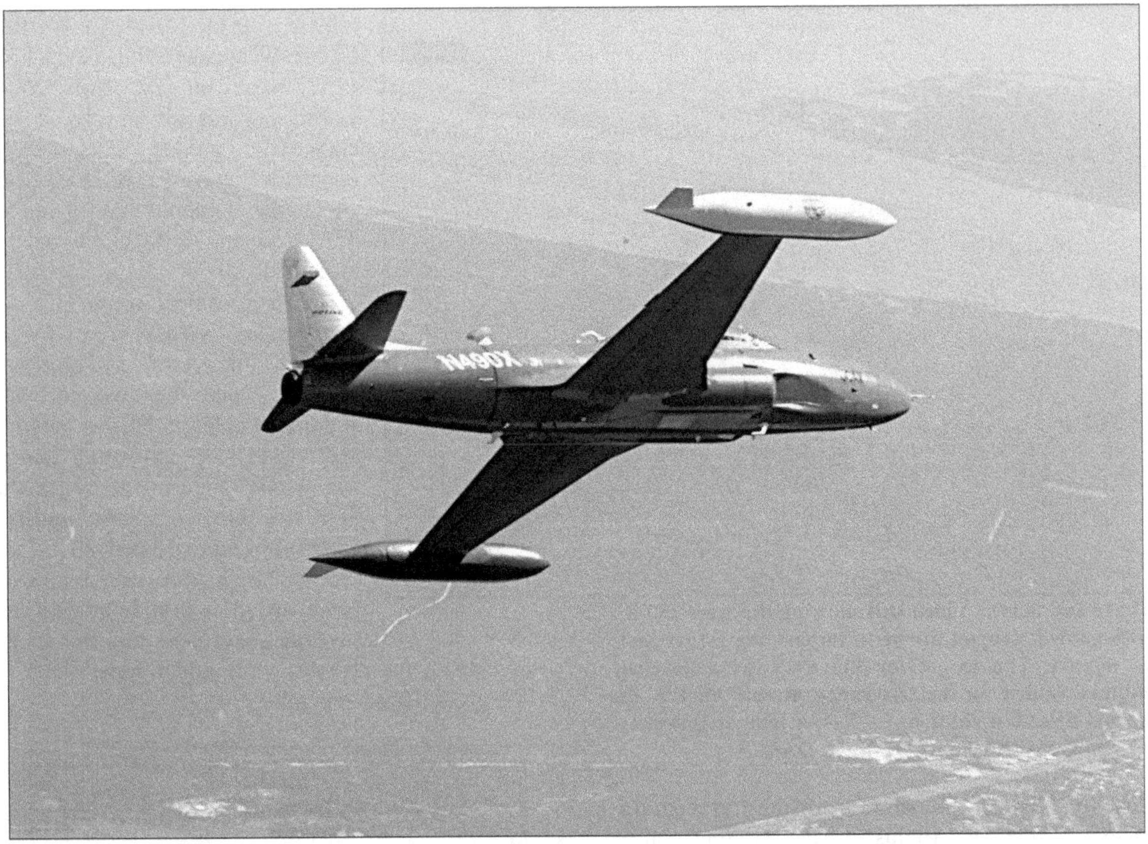
N490X

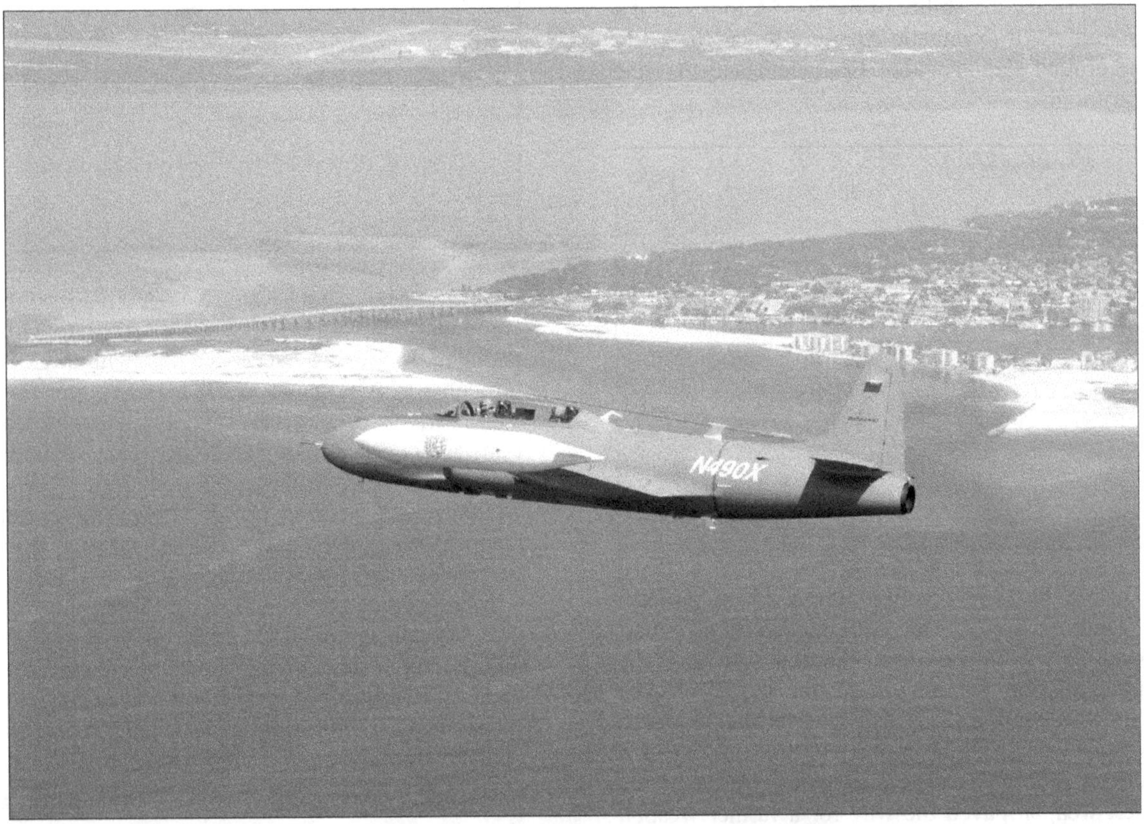
N490X

Previous page: In May 2004 an X-45A successfully communicated with a T-33 UCAV surrogate while in-flight. The two aircraft exchanged data through a system known as the FDL (Fighter Data Link); a secure data link allowing the transfer of electronic data between different platforms. Above: AV-1 and AV-2 on the ramp at Edwards AFB. DARPA

knots. During the trials both X-45A's maintained their positions relative to each other through the inter-vehicle data link.

The joint flight-tests got underway on 1 August 2004 at Edwards with the first mission with both X-45A's under the control of a single-pilot operator in a coordinated flight. The Two X-45A's took-off from Edwards in succession, four minutes apart, before joining-up over the test range. During the flight the 2 X-45A's flew a series of preset formations, which involved the vehicles conducting autonomous manoeuvring in order to maintain their relative positions. The air vehicles flew the same "mission plan" individually, reducing the workload of the ground based pilot operator. The test mission was conducted at 14,500-ft altitude for AV-1 and 15,000-ft for AV-2 with the X-45 flying at airspeed of Mach 0.6 (around 390 mph). Lateral separation of over 1 mile was maintained between the two vehicles during the flight. Information concerning aircraft status was shared between the 2 X-45A's via the Link 16 data link. The air vehicles landed back at Edwards on the same runway ending the mission after around 40-minutes in the air. Operational missions involving an operational UCAV are envisioned to include up to four vehicles controlled by a single ground based pilot operator, while flying in closer formations to that conducted in the 1 August 2004 trial.

The X-45A mission control station at St Louis looks much like an industry workstation. Boeing

Previous page: While the X-45A vehicles were given an unprecedented degree of autonomy, the human-in-the-loop capability allowed the ground-based pilot-controller to take control of the vehicle at any point had the need arose. Boeing **Above:** As the flight-test program progressed, the need for AV-2 became apparent with the move to multi-vehicle flights. **Left:** One of the X-45A vehicles on the ramp at Edwards. The thrust-vectoring engine exhaust nozzle has been closed-off. DARPA

Taxi tests of the X-45A with the Block 3 software were conducted at Edwards in August and September 2004 and flight-testing the Block 3 software began on 21 October with the X-45A's 36th flight, with a further flight conducted on 28 October. The 21 October flight verified that the single-ship capability, demonstrated with previous software blocks, worked correctly with the Block 3 software. The Block 3 software allowed the X-45A's to fly autonomously co-ordinated missions and engage one target. With Block 4 software the vehicles would be capable of flying autonomously co-ordinated missions and engage multiple targets.

The flight on 28 October was the 37th X-45A flight and the first test of the X-45A's ability to quickly respond to "a changing environment." During the flight, the Automated Dynamic Mission Planning system responded to a simulated ground-threat by plotting a new route to avoid the threat and sending the data back to the pilot operator at the ground station and re-routing the vehicle onto the new course once the pilot operator agreed and

UCAV
DARPA
BOEING PHANTOM WORKS

UCAV
DARPA
BOEING PHANTOM WORKS

Previous page top: An X-45A lands back at Edwards AFB following a UCAV development test flight. Boeing **Previous page bottom: An X-45 sits on the ramp at Edwards on 21 March 2004. Note the open exhaust area. Above: X-45A AV-1 is seen getting airborne at Edwards in 2002.** Boeing **Right: X-45A AV-1 is shadowed by chase aircraft, F-18B #846, during a test flight.** DARPA

sent the data back to the vehicle. Once the threat had been successfully avoided the X-45A resumed its original course to resume the attack mission.

On 12 November 2004, the 2 X-45A's conducted their first multi-vehicle flight using the Block 3 software, demonstrating the "4-d" navigation allowing the two X-45As to control their arrival time over a designated geographical position as well as maintaining relative position. The next multi-vehicle flight was conducted on 3 December when the X-45A's flew in several formations, demonstrating the UCAV systems ability to conducted autonomous entry and exit of coordinated flight based on previously identified waypoints as well as the ability to dynamically alter the formation "in all three axis simultaneously."

A pilot operator at a control station controlled an X-45A after take-off Edwards on 9 December 2004. This flight was aimed at demonstrating

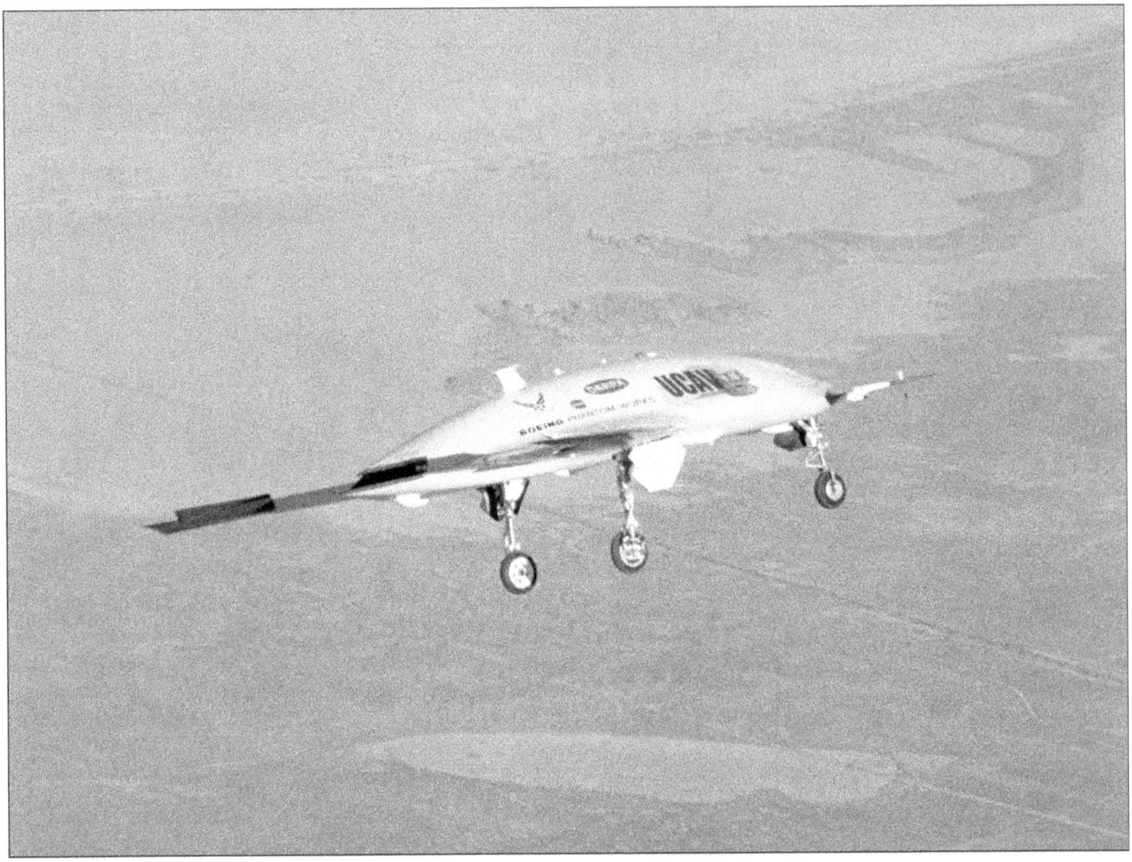
UCAV

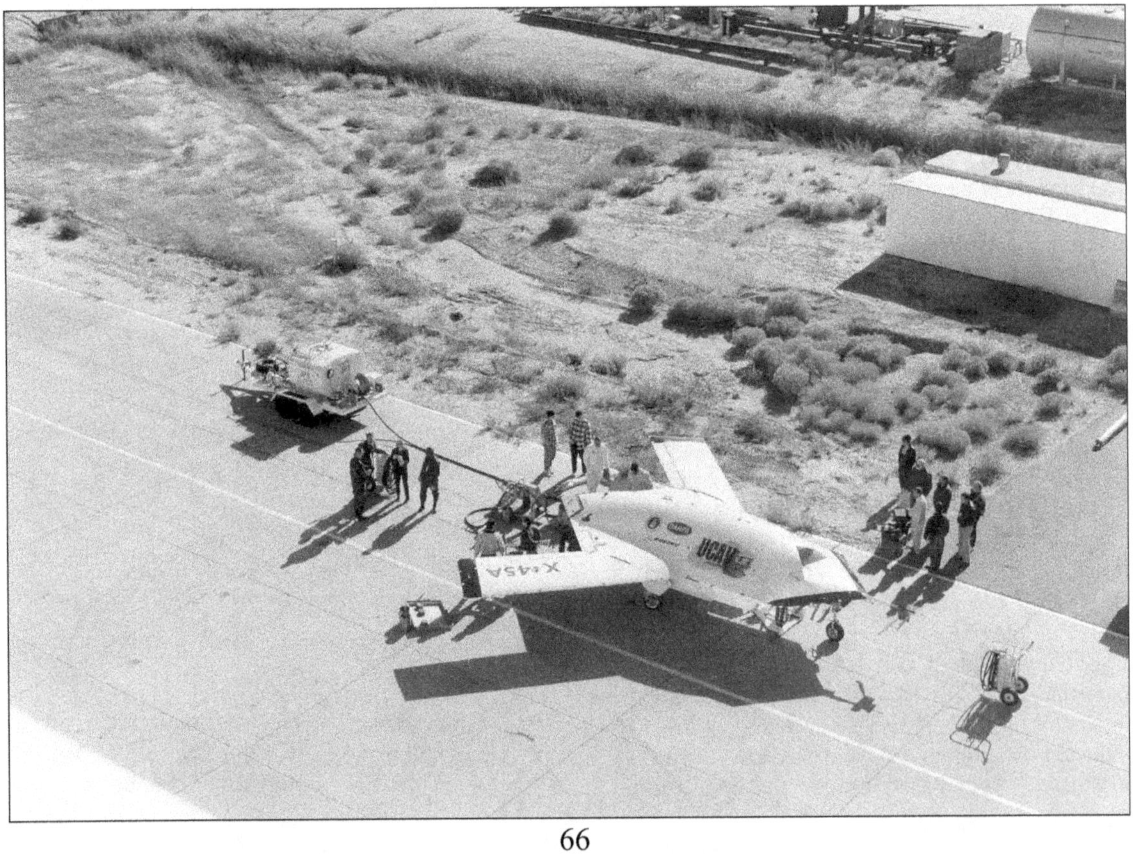
X-45A
UCAV

Previous page top: X-45A AV-1 is seen in a gentle turn to port westbound south of the 'racetrack' at Edwards AFB. Previous page bottom: Ground crew perform a hot refuelling on AV-1 with the engine running. This page: The NASA F-18B Hornet chase aircraft casts its shadow on the runway at Edwards AFB as an X-45A conducts its landing roll in the background. All Boeing

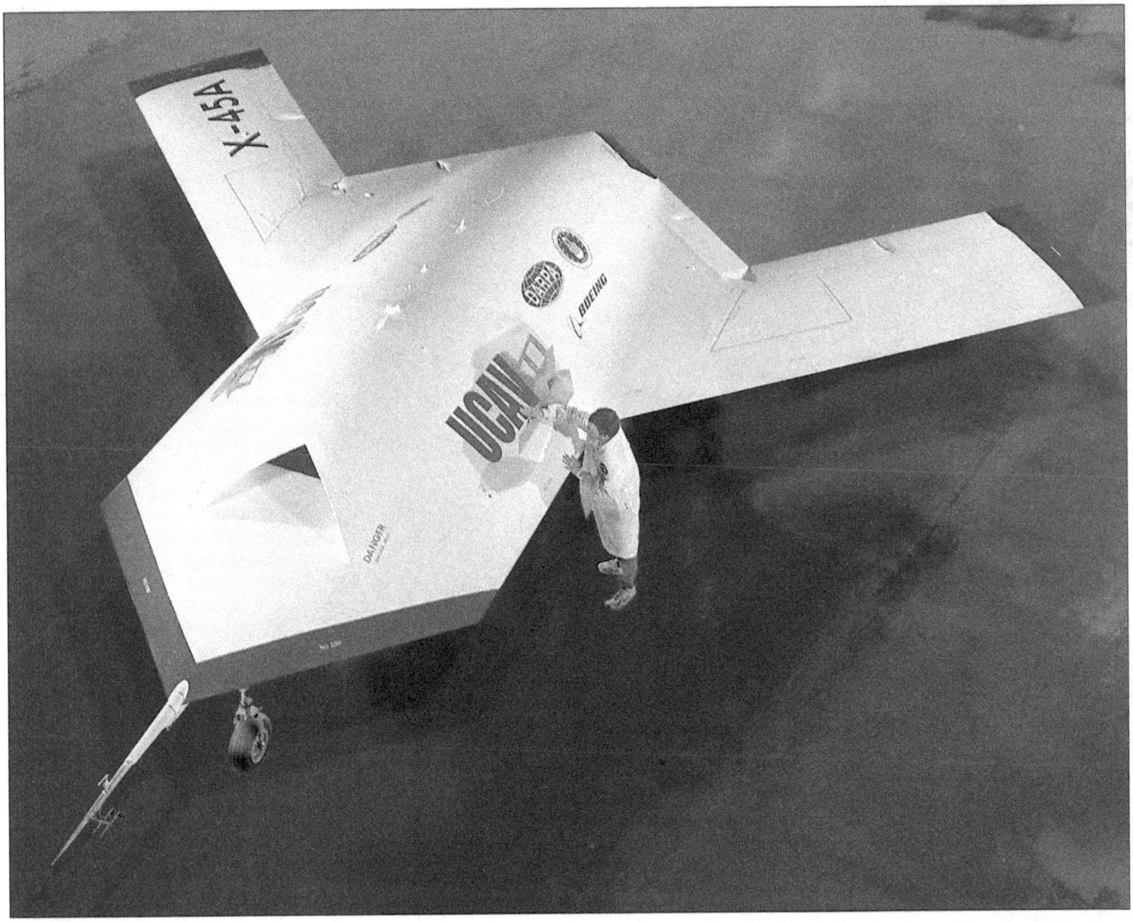
X-45A
UCAV
BOEING
DANGER

UCAV
BOEING PHANTOM WORKS

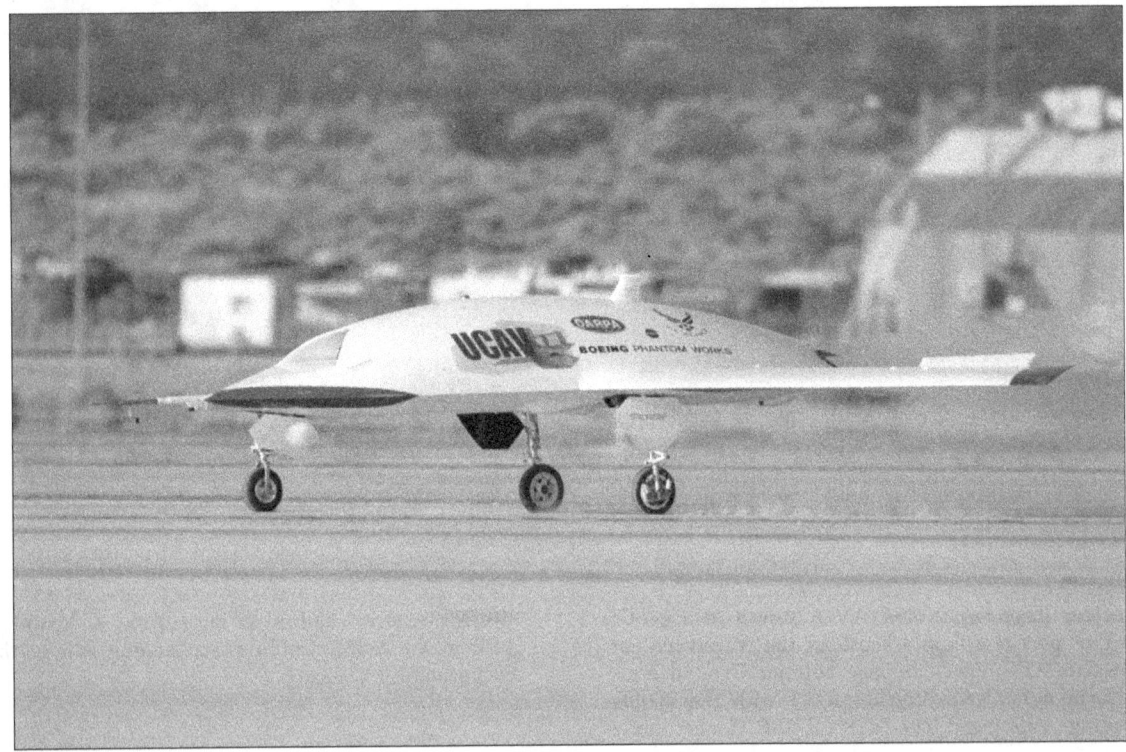

Previous page top: The X-45A was never intended to be a definitive design for an operational system, being much smaller than that planned for an operational variant. Boeing Previous page bottom: The second X-45A, AV-2, begins its take-off roll at Edwards. NASA DFRC This page: The two X-45A's conducted their first simulated combat mission on 5 February 2005. The aircraft before the mission (top) and AV-2 landing back at Edwards AFB (bottom). Boeing

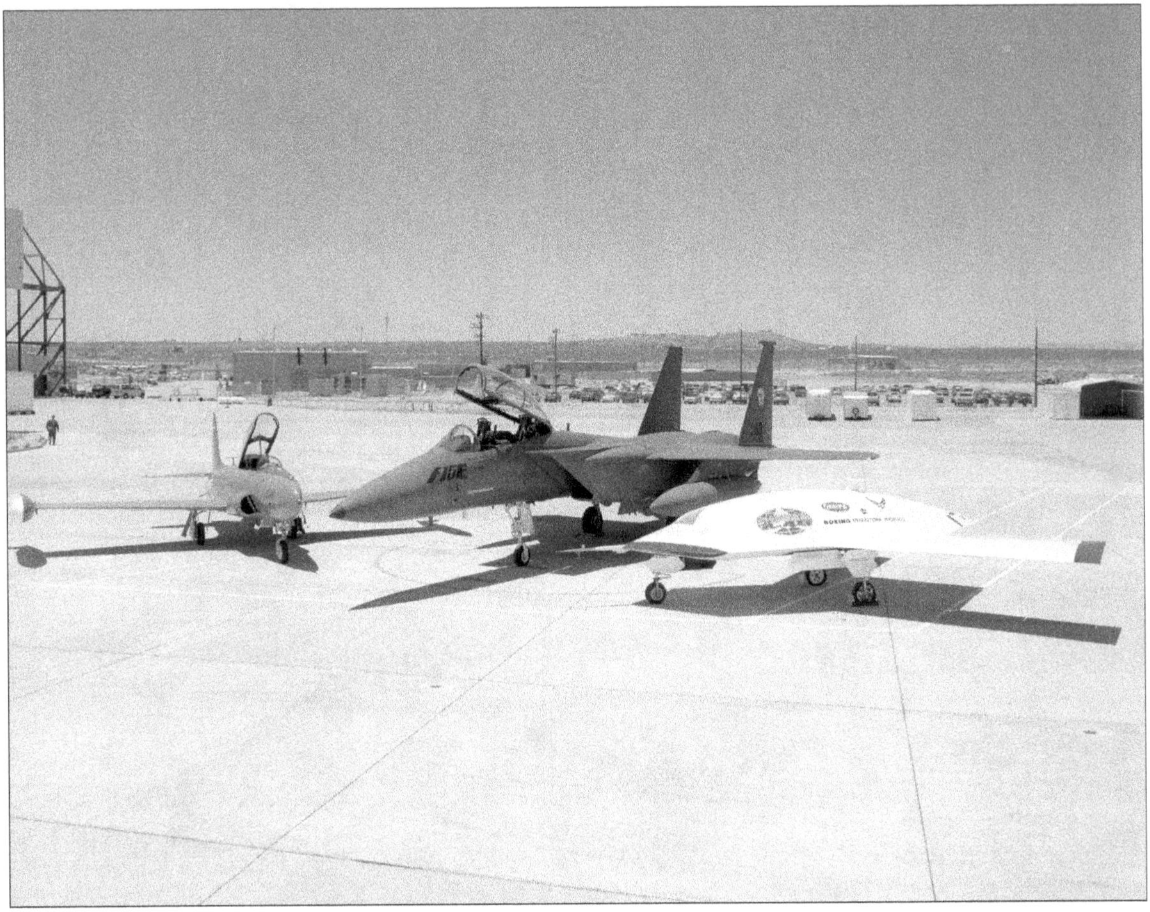

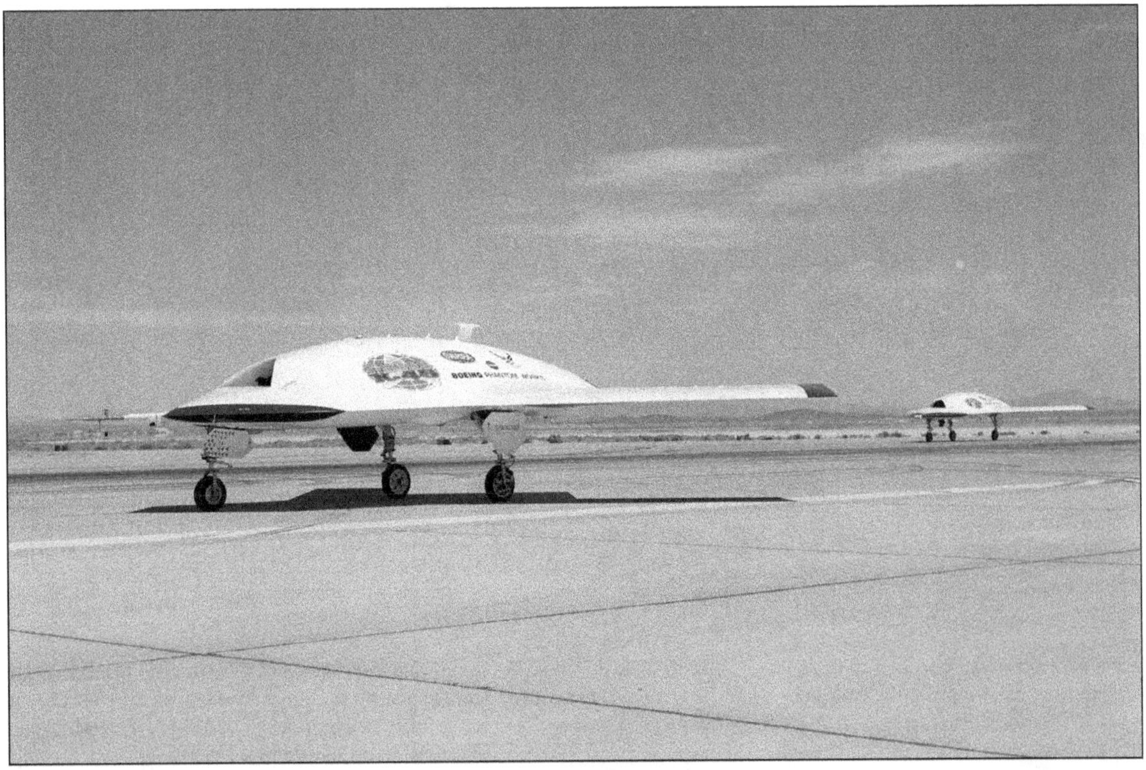

Previous page top: In June 2004, SEC flight tests were conducted using the T-33 UCAV surrogate and the first Boeing F-15E, E1, which is used by Boeing as an advanced technology demonstrator. The T-33 and F-15E1 are parked alongside X-45A AV-2 at Edwards AFB. Previous page bottom and this page: AV-1 leads AV-2 as the vehicles taxi for take-off during Block 3 software testing in early 2005. All Boeing

An X-45A banks to starboard during its initial climb following take-off from Edwards AFB. Boeing

that a UCAV flying from one location could be controlled by an operator at a different location. Control of the flight was conducted using line of sight and control. The X-45A took-off from Dryden under control of an operator at Dryden. Once the aircraft was airborne, control was handed over to an operator at Boeings Seattle facility. Line of sight command and control of the vehicle was conducted using a UHF (Ultra High Frequency) SATCOM (Satellite Communications) link with the X-45A being controlled through multiple altitude and airspeed changes during the flight. The pilot operator at Seattle controlled the X-45A for around 6-minuets before handing control back to the pilot operator at Dryden almost 900 miles away. Under Dryden control the X-45A was then landed back at Edwards after being airborne for almost one hour. During the flight the Seattle based ground control pilot sent four airspeed and altitude command alterations to the X-45A.

On 27 January 2005, a transfer of command and control using line-of-sight of the two X-45A's was successfully demonstrated during Block 3 testing, designed to demonstrate the tactical utility of the X-45's command and control capability by passing control of the vehicles from the primary ground control pilot to a ground control pilot in the area of operations. Once the secondary ground control pilot has manoeuvred the vehicles to conduct the mission, such as capturing images, command and control is then passed back to the primary ground control pilot.

For the test, the secondary ground control pilot was located only around 100-ft from the primary ground control pilot at NASA Dryden at Edwards, but he tactical flexibility of the distributed command and control system was aptly demonstrated. Throughout the flight-test both X-45A's remained within Edwards AFB airspace.

The 2 X-45A's flew a simulated combat mission on 4 February 2005, during which the programs 50th X-45 flight was achieved. The mission known as 'Peacekeeper' began when both X-45A's

X-45A AV-2 is seen from above during the final X-45A mission of the flight-test program in August 2005. Boeing

departed Edwards AFB and climbed to altitudes of 24,500-ft and 25,500-ft respectively. The two vehicles were flying around 25 miles apart at airspeed of Mach 0.65 (225-kts). The aircraft were tasked to fly an orbit over an exercise area tasked with providing SEAD. During the mission the 2 X-45's were given two simulated "pop-up ground based threats." Once the first threat – a simulated ground based radar system- was detected, the 2 X-45A's autonomously decided which of the two vehicles was best positioned to strike the target. Once the decision had been made the X-45A selected to deal with the threat-changed course and the ground-based pilot operator then allowed the vehicle to attack the simulated target. Once this was completed another simulated threat was handed to the X-45A's and this was attacked by the second X-45A. With the mission over the 2 X-45A's returned to Edwards AFB.

Before the test mission was flown, the program conducted a long software integration and test phase with the software for the 'Peacekeeper' test flight undergoing over 2,800 hours of testing in the high-fidelity SIL (System Integration Laboratory). Flight testing in the Lockheed T-33 UCAV surrogate further refined the software. This testing built on data gathered from DARPA's SEC (Software Enabled Control) program, which began in the 1990's with the goal of simulating new concepts for autonomous uninhabited air vehicles, which rely on multiple on-board models. Technology from this program fed into the UCAV and later J-UCAS programs.

In June 2004, SEC flight tests were conducted using the T-33 UCAV surrogate and the first Boeing F-15E, E1, which was used by Boeing as an advanced technology demonstrator. The flight tests successfully demonstrated the emerging autonomous control technologies designed to allow real-time collision avoidance, the ability of a UCAV to conduct autonomous evasive manoeuvres and conduct autonomous re-routing when faced with an unexpected pop-up threat or an in-flight fault.

Boeing began flight-testing the block 4 software during the 51st X-45A flight on 13 May 2005. This flight was preceded by a series of ground tests including taxi trials of the vehicle fitted with Block 4 software during April and early May 2005. The 13 May flight successfully demonstrated that basic command and control functionality, which had been demonstrated in previous software blocks, functioned correctly with the block 4 software. During the flight, the X-45A reached an altitude of 15,000-ft and a speed of Mach 0.40. The block 4 software was put forward by Boeing as a candidate for functionality during the development of the J-UCAS COS (Common Operating System).

The block 4 software was designed to demonstrate the ability of the X-45A to autonomously attack target and react to "dynamic changes in the threat environment", therefore, the new software tests paved the way for the final X-45A demonstrations in August 2005.

This final demonstration test series would see the X-45A's fly what was described as their most challenging simulated combat mission at that time. The mission was the 63rd and 64th X-45A flights. The mission scenario saw the 2 X-45A's take-off from Edwards and climb to the operating altitude and use their own decision making software to determine the appropriate route within the confines of the AOA (Area OF Action). Once the vehicles software selected the route the ground-based pilot controller approved the decision following which the 2 X-45A's moved into the AOA, which was a 30-mile by 60-mile area of the test range. The X-45A's then continued with the mission – a simulated pre-emptive destruction of and air defence target. The mission scenario required the X-45A's to identify, attack and destroy the pre-identified surface target, which for the mission was a simulated radar system with associated SAM (surface to Air Missile) launch system. The requirement of the mission was for the target to be destroyed before any simulated SAM's could be launched.

The mission also saw a simulated pop-up threat being introduced, requiring the X-45A to take evasive manoeuvring action to avoid the threat while autonomously deciding which of the two vehicles was in the optimum position, with weapons and fuel to strike the highest priority simulated target. Following authorisation from the ground based pilot controller, the X-45A's simulated a weapons drop on the target before engaging a second simulated pop-up threat following which the vehicles returned to Edwards AFB.

The successful conclusion of this mission effectively concluded the X-45A flight demonstration program paving the way for the more advanced and challenging X-45C program.

During the flight demonstration program the two X-45A vehicles successfully demonstrated the 'basic functionality' of the C3 and navigation systems as well as proving the aerodynamic configuration and demonstrating the systems ability to fly autonomously using pre-programmed digital mission plans and the ability of ground controllers to communicate and change mission scenarios in flight.

Boeing X-45A

Length: 26.5-ft
Fuselage length: 26.3-ft
Height: 3.7-ft
Span: 33.8-ft
Empty weight: 8,000-lb
Fuel volume: 2,960-lb
Payload: 1,500-lb
Operating altitude: 10670-m (35,000-ft)
Cruise speed: Mach 0.80
Engine: Honeywell F124-GA-100

Chapter Three

Northrop Grumman X-47A 'Pegasus'

The private venture Northrop Grumman 'Pegasus' UCAV demonstrator was allocated the 'X-47' designation and integrated into the wider UCAV-N program in June 2001. The vehicles small size is apparent in this forward view. Northrop Grumman

While DARPA/Boeing and the USAF were pushing ahead with the X-45A UCAV ATD (Advanced Technology Demonstrator) program, attention was beginning to refocus on a viable UCAV capable of operating from the decks of aircraft carriers for use by the USN, which planned to operate such vehicles alongside conventional inhabited fighter aircraft. While the X-45A was intended as a UCAV demonstrator for a USAF program, the DARPA/USN UCAV-N (Uninhabited Combat Air Vehicle-Naval) was focused mainly on system studies for operation from an aircraft carrier. Northrop Grumman embarked had upon its Pegasus program as a private venture, which yielded the single X-47A demonstrator, which although independently funded and built by Northrop Grumman, was flight-tested under the auspices of the UCAV-N program, which was later absorbed into the J-UCAS program.

On 30 June 2000, DARPA and the USN awarded contracts for the first phase of the UCAV-N ATD program. Northrop Grumman and Boeing each received $2 million contracts to conduct the initial 15 month study, analysis and the preliminary design phase of the program. The main goal of the UCAV-N program was the demonstration of the technical feasibility of effectively and affordably operating a UCAV-N platform from aircraft carriers to conduct a variety of missions including SEAD, strike and surveillance within the increasingly sophisticated global command and control architecture. The main function of the Pegasus demonstrations was to test low-speed handling, simulated arrested landings at a shore base and demonstration of an avionics and vehicle management system, which was developed by BAE Systems.

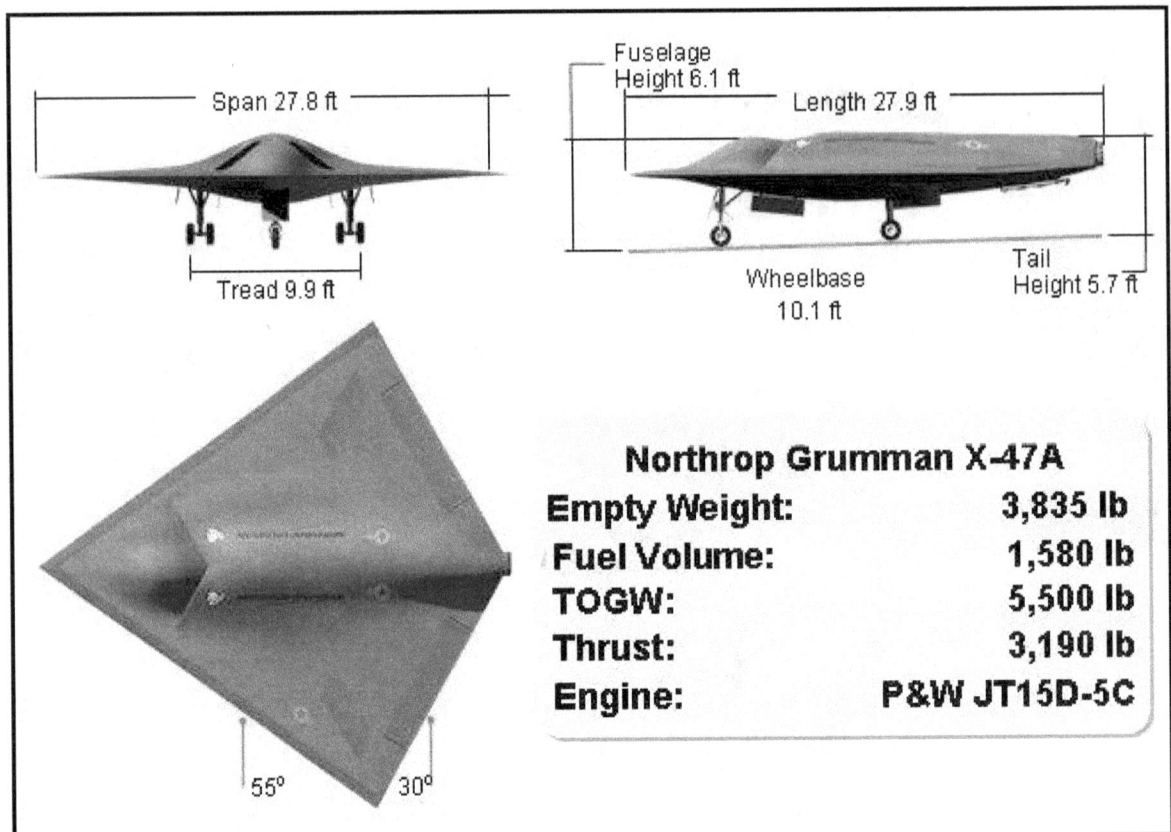

3-view General arrangement drawing of the X-47A. DARPA

With Boeing benefiting from experience and technology developed for the X-45A ATD program, Northrop Grumman was in danger of being left behind. Therefore, in July 2000, Northrop Grumman took the decision to privately fund construction of an UCAV-N demonstrator air vehicle, which it named Pegasus. Objectives of the Pegasus program were to demonstrate low-speed aerodynamic handling qualities; compatibility with aircraft carrier landing systems; simulated landing arrestment and to demonstrate an air vehicle management and architecture which could be applicable to future UAV/UCAV's.

The Pegasus design was formally unveiled by Northrop Grumman in February 2001. The design drew on advanced technologies developed at the company's Advanced Systems Development Centre in El Segundo, California. Construction of the Pegasus air vehicle was completed by 30 July 2001. On that date the Pegasus, which had received the X-47A designation at the Paris Air Salon on 16 June, was rolled out of its assembly hanger at Mojave, California and a full-scale model of the vehicle was displayed at Air Demonstration 2001 at NAS (Naval Air Station) Patuxent River, Maryland.

The X-46 designation had been allocated to a planned Boeing UCAV-N demonstration program and it was also revealed that a larger variant more closely resembling an operational UCAV-N concept would receive the designation X-47B.

The X-47A was built for Northrop Grumman at Scaled Composites, Mojave California. Built mainly from composite materials, the vehicle was designed with stealth features to reduce the already small radar signature. The aircraft, which has an empty weight of 3,835-lb, was powered by a single Pratt & Whitney Canada JT15D-5C turbofan engine, rated at 3,190-lb thrust. Maximum take-off weight was 5,500-lb. Length was 27.9-ft with a wingspan of 27.8-ft. The more or less identical length and span create a more or less 'kite' shape. The aircraft featured autonomous flight control laws to account for directional control of the tailless design and was equipped with a 'next generation' carrier landing-system known as the SRGPS (Ship-board Relative Global Positioning System). As well as the X-47A flight vehicle Northrop Grumman built the associated mission control, support and simulation systems.

The X-47A 'Pegasus' is getting airborne on its 12 minute maiden flight in February 2003. The name Pegasus denotes the winged horse of ancient Greek mythology Northrop Grumman

With the air vehicle complete the X-47A entered a program of ground testing in preparation for its maiden flight and conducted its first engine-run in December 2001 followed by the second run in January 2002. The third engine-run was conducted on 16 March 2002 as the program progressed towards the first autonomous engine-run. Other work included avionics integration conducted at the systems integration laboratory El Segundo. Once systems checkout had been completed the X-47A was transferred to China Lake to conduct taxi trials, with the first low-speed taxi test being conducted on 19 July 2002, demonstrating the initial capability of the vehicles command and control, navigation, steering performance and operation of the brakes. On 6 September 2002, the X-47A successfully conducted its second low-speed taxi-test, demonstrating integrated navigation and control as well as steering performance as the vehicle was turned onto the runway and then taxied down in a zigzag pattern.

The taxi tests paved the way for the X-47A's maiden flight, which was conducted on 23 February 2003 when the X-47A lifted-off from China Lake, at approximately 07:56 PST. The aircraft flew for 12-minutes before landing at a pre-designated touchdown point required to simulate the tail-hook arrestment wire point on an aircraft carrier deck. During the flight, low-speed handling qualities, air vehicle performance, navigation performance and collection of landing dispersion data were conducted successfully. This, together with later landings was aimed at demonstrating the X-47A's landing accuracy. Increased precision on landing was aided by the use of the shipboard-relative GPS system as the primary navigation source. Like the Global Hawk and Fire Scout UAV's, the X-47A conducted its first flight "from engine start to shutdown, without human intervention." During the maiden flight the test team detected slight oscillation at a speed of 130-kts (240-kmh). The X-47A program aimed to successfully conduct precision approaches at 110-knots at descent angles up to 4-degrees using the shipboard relative GPS.

The X-47 sits on the ramp at sunset. However, the sun was rising on the UCAV concept, which would lead to larger more capable UCAV's developed under the J-UCAS program. Northrop Grumman

During the first approach landing, the X-47A had a dispersion of 2.4-m (18-ft) in length and 4.9-m lateral of the pre designated touchdown point. Landing the X-47A close to a pre-designated touchdown point successfully simulated a tail-hook arrestment. The shipboard-relative GPS system was used as the primary navigation source allowing a precise landing.

While the X-47A program was much lower key than the X-45A program, by early 2003, Northrop Grumman had invested in excess of $40 million in the Pegasus program with DARPA and the USN contributing $5.6 million. As the UCAV-N program moved on. Northrop Grumman was awarded a contract modification in May 2002. This contract, which was valued at $10 million covered additional risk-reduction and technology studies, which included modelling work and simulation of autonomous flight operations from an aircraft carrier.

In late summer 2004, the full-scale model of the X-47A was loaned to the Naval Air Museum for display at Patuxent River, Maryland.

X-47A Pegasus

Length: 27.9-ft
Wingspan: 27.9-ft
Empty weight: 3,835-lb
Fuel volume: 1,580-lb
TOGW: 5,500-lb
Engine: P&W Canada JT15D-5C developing 3,190-lb thrust

Prior to its first flight, the Pegasus vehicle conducted a series of taxi tests paving the way for the successful maiden flight. Northrop Grumman

Chapter Four

Joint-Uninhabited Combat Air System and Beyond

The X-45C was developed into the Boeing Phantom Ray, which conducted its first flight in April 2011. Boeing

The J-UCAS (Joint-Uninhabited Combat Air System) program was born when it absorbed the DARPA/USAF UCAV and DARPA/USN UCAV-N programs, which were being conducted separately with the aim of demonstrating technologies for possible armed uninhabited air vehicles for the USAF and USN. Combining the UCAV and UCAV-N efforts into one program was aimed at reducing costs and duplication of development. The J-UCAS program office officially took over the two programs on 1 October 2003, with its headquarters located at DARPA facilities in Arlington, Virginia and with personnel operating from the AFASC (Air Forces Aeronautical Systems Centre) in Dayton, Ohio and from the NASC (Naval Air Systems Command) located at Patuxent River, Maryland.

The program was a joint program by DARPA, the USAF and the USN whose goal was to successfully demonstrate "the technical feasibility, military utility and operational value of a network system of high performance, armed uninhabited air vehicles to effectively and affordably prosecute 21st Century combat missions including SEAD; Electronic Attack; precision strike; surveillance; reconnaissance and persistence global attack within the emerging global command and control architecture."

While both the UCAV and UCAV-N programs were aimed at different objectives, enough common ground existed for a joint program to be launched. A number of common mission requirements were set forward including a radius of 1,300 nm; persistence 1,000 nm with a 2-hour loiter capability and a payload of 4,500-lb. The land based and carrier based UCAV developments faced similar technical challenges including the need to develop an affordable, stealthy UCAV "capable of dynamic distributed control using advanced cognitive aids and advanced targeting processes." A major requirement for both services was that the J-UCAS be fully interoperable with inhabited aircraft and other air vehicles.

Initial planning was for the X-45A to lead to a larger variant designated X-45B, to demonstrate technologies applicable to an operational variant. This rendering shows an operational UCAV based on the X-45A design operating in a mixed formation of UCAV's and F-15E Eagle strike aircraft. Boeing

Left: Boeing had embarked upon development of the X-46 as the basis for its UCAV-N concept. With the changing requirements of the UCAV and UCAV-N programs, the programs would eventually be merged into a single common airframe program. Boeing

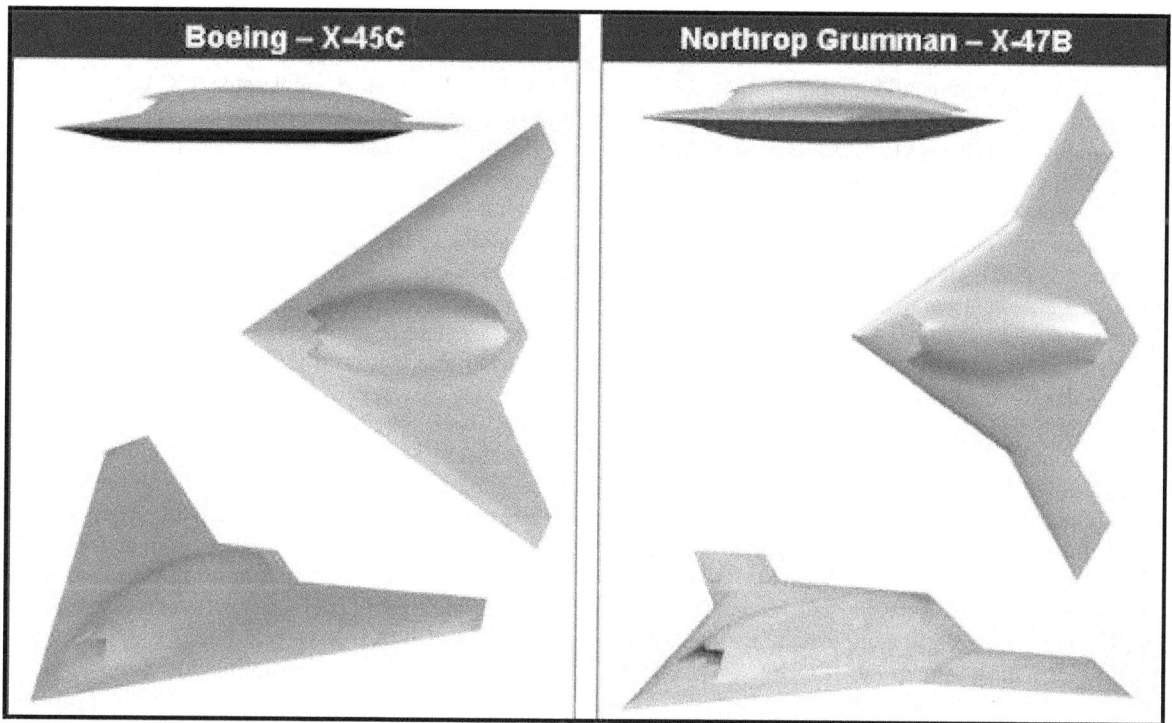

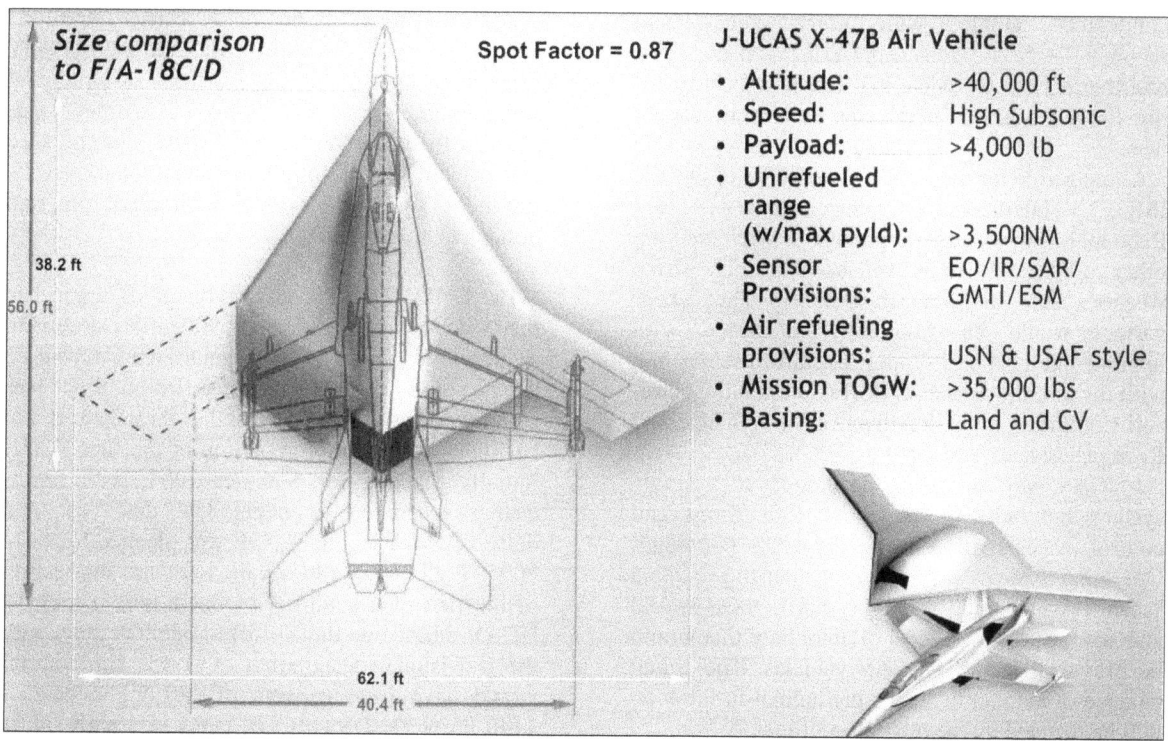

Top: When designing the Boeing X-45C and Northrop Grumman X-47B J-UCAS vehicles, both contractors arrived at similar solutions to similar problems. Therefore, both air vehicles are remarkably similar in overall layout, size and weight. DARPA Above: This diagram shows the size comparison of the X-47B compared with the Boeing F/A-18C Hornet inhabited strike fighter, which is typical of a standard current generation naval strike fighter. Northrop Grumman

The initial role for an operational USAF segment of the J-UCAS was described as a "first day of war" UCAV, which would support other UAV's and uninhabited combat aircraft by conducting both lethal and non-lethal SEAD (Suppression of Enemy Air Defence). The J-UCAS would be equipped to conduct electronic suppression and pre-emptive destruction of an enemy IADS (Integrated Air Defence System) clearing a route for inhabited aircraft. Later in a campaign the USAF J-UCAS variant would be required to conduct surveillance and provide an immediate strike capability against "high value" and time critical targets. This would be accomplished by J-UCAS vehicles loitering in the operational area awaiting targeting details being handed down from other platforms or locating and identifying the targets autonomously.

The initial operational role envisioned for the USN J-UCAS would be to provide a highly survivable, persistent surveillance, reconnaissance and targeting capability, complementing inhabited aircraft operating alongside it. The USN also envisioned the use of long-range strike weapons for its J-UCAS. The strike and SEAD roles being conducted along with surveillance and reconnaissance are considered critical to the USN requirement for a vehicle that can pay its way for the limited space available on an aircraft carrier deck.

A major role for the J-UCAS would be electronic ISR (Intelligence Surveillance and Reconnaissance) and targeting, complementing other airborne assets as well as long-range strike weapons such as stand-off missiles. The carrier variant would be seamlessly integrated with inhabited combat and support aircraft missions and with the aircraft carriers C4ISR (Command Control and Communications Intelligence Surveillance and Reconnaissance) architecture.

J-UCAS was not being developed as a single system, but rather a collection of platforms and control systems all utilising the COS (Common Operating System) and linked together to provide a "seamless integrated capability." The COS would also manage the high level of autonomy that would be prevalent in the J-UCAS vehicles. The actual balance of autonomy versus the human-in-the-loop will be dictated by the mission profile.

Although going through the inevitable program name changes, the program led to the Boeing X-45B, which was developed further into the X-45C. The program also led to the Northrop Grumman X-47B. The J-UCAS development program was to be conducted in a series of increasingly more capable overlapping Spirals, planned to culminate in the objective system. Spiral 0 consisted of the two Boeing X-45A and the single Northrop Grumman X-47A Pegasus demonstrator UCAV's and all associated systems including ground control stations once these programs had been Absorbed into the J-UCAS program The X-45A segment of Spiral 0 also included the development and testing of software Blocks 1 to 4, each more capable than the previous.

Spiral 1 consisted of among other things the development of improved UCAV demonstrators by Boeing and Northrop Grumman designated X-45C and X-47B respectively. These vehicles are larger than their predecessors and incorporate more advanced technology including low-observable technology and are designed to more closely represent the planned operational configuration. The larger size also allows more fuel and weapons load to be carried and more powerful engines increasing overall performance over the smaller X-45A and X-47A.

Spiral 1 objective was to include demonstrations of land-based catapult launches and arrested landings, taxi operations from land surfaces and deck operations on-board a carrier and the demonstration of low-cost low-observable technologies. Following the Spiral 1 demonstrations, an operational assessment was planned for fiscal year 2007 to determine the need and capabilities of follow-on operational systems for the USAF/USN, with a number of program options to be presented a few years later.

The X-45B was to be around one third larger than the X-45A with a radius of 900 miles and a 30 minute loiter over the operational area carrying up to 12 SDB (Small Diameter Bombs). It was planned for two, later increased to three X-45B's to be flight-tested with completion of the first X-45B initially planned for Summer 2004; with flight-testing scheduled to begin late that year and delivery of the second X-45B was planned for early 2005. Preliminary plans called for the fabrication of the first of a batch of 14 operational Block 10 UCAV's based on the X-45B to begin in 2006 with the provisional designation of A-45. This variant would have been capable of carrying a pair of 1140-litre (300 US gal) fuel tanks externally under the wings. Payloads would have included a pair of MALD (Miniature Air Launched Decoy), a pair of JDAM (Joint Direct Attack Munitions) up to 12 SDB or an auxiliary fuel tank fitted in the internal weapons bay. Planned combinations included 8 SDB and a pair of 450-kg JDAM's.

While the X-45B was aimed at demonstrating technologies for a land based UCAV, Boeing commenced development of the X-46 concept to demonstrate technologies for the UCAV-N program. Prior to embarking upon the X-46 program, Boeing put forward a lower-cost lower-risk study to the USN. Boeings proposal was to demonstrate the UCAV-N aircraft carrier compatibility and capabilities using a Boeing F/A-18 Hornet strike fighter as a piloted UCAV-N surrogate together with a full-scale UCAV-N vehicle for ground testing including evaluation of deck handling and accommodation.

While Boeing embarked upon the X-45B/C and X-46 programs, Northrop Grumman embarked upon the X-47B program, the main focus of which was the naval UCAV portion of what would become the J-UCAS program, although the USAF segment was added later as both services requirements moved closer. The X-47B adopted the cranked 'kite' layout directly descendent from the smaller X-47A. However, the X-47B design added winglets to improve the vehicles low-speed handling qualities and endurance. The X-47B, which was at the larger end of the UCAV scale, was to weigh over 42,000-lb and have a 4,500-lb payload. As the design iterations progressed Northrop Grumman unveiled its X-47B concept for an operational UCAV in April 2003. The new design combined some features of the smaller X-47A's 'kite' aerodynamic configuration with a flying wing design.

In response to USAF concerns that the X-45B would lack range and payload capability for some mission scenarios, Boeing began offering the larger X-45C variant to the USAF in January 2003. The X-45C had emerged following concerns that the X-45B would not meet the changing operational requirements. By April 2003, DARPA had formally requested that Boeing modify the X-45B design to meet different operational requirements to that previously laid-down when the X-45B concept was evolving, therefore, the X-45C now assumed pre-eminence in the Boeing UCAV range. DARPA and the USAF changed the operational requirement to include greater payload, range and persistence requiring a change of design from that put forward for the X-45B. These changes also allowed the USAF UCAV and USN UCAV-N requirements to move closer to a common program with the X-45C now forming the basis of the Boeing UCAV-N proposal leaving the X-46 concept in limbo.

The X-45C is based on the centre body and sub-systems of the X-45B, but also incorporating a new planform designed to carry more fuel as well as providing improved aerodynamic performance. The increased fuel capacity gave the X-45C three times more combat radius than that planned for the X-45B while carrying the same payload. The X-45C does, however, have a larger payload than that planned for the X-45B.

Under the auspices of the J-UCAS program, the X-47B and X-45C designs increased in weight as additional capabilities and versatility were incorporated into the program. By 2004 the projected weight of the X-45C was around 17250-kg. By autumn 2004, Northrop Grumman's X-47B design had grown to a weight of 21790-kg and the design team embarked upon a weight reduction program aimed at reducing overall weight by around 5900-kg (13,000-lb).

The X-47A conducted its maiden flight on 4 February 2011, by which time the program had been renamed UCAS-D. The X-45C flagged and them was revived as the Boeing Phantom Ray UAS (Unmanned Airborne System), conducting its first flight on 27 April 2011. Northrop Grumman added a second X-47B to the UCAS-D program when this aircraft conducted its first flight at Patuxent River, Maryland in July 2012.

The Phantom Ray/X-47B vehicles will demonstrate the feasibility of an operational UCAV system in a modern air combat environment including the ability to operate within mixed formations consisting of inhabited and uninhabited aircraft. The UCAS-D program is investigating simulated carrier operations using the JPALS (Joint Precision Approach Landing System). Over the next decade or so UCAV concepts and operations will increasingly become a reality as not just the United States, but many other nations, particularly in Europe, continue studies and demonstrations aimed at increasing maturity of such systems so that they will one day be capable of operating in airspace used by inhabited systems.

Boeing X-45B

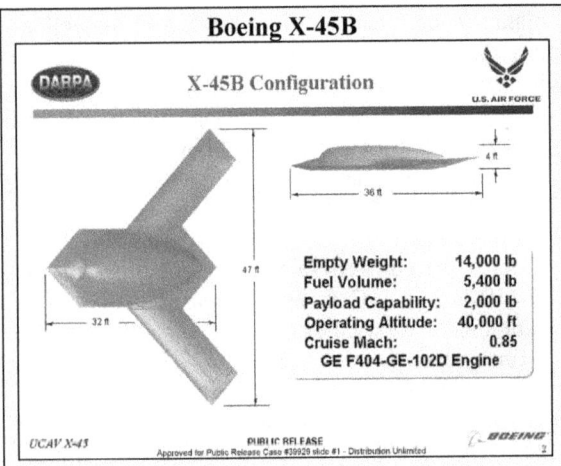

Length: 36-ft overall; fuselage length 32-ft
Height: 4-ft
Span: 47-ft
Empty weight: 14,000-lb
Fuel volume: 5,400-lb
Payload: 2,000-lb
Operating altitude: 40,000-ft
Cruise speed: Mach 0.85
Engine: General Electric F404-GE-102D

Northrop Grumman X-47B

Length: 38.2 ft
Wingspan: 62.1 ft
Range: 2,100 nm
Top Speed: High Subsonic
Maximum ceiling: 12-km (40,000-ft)
Combat radius: 1,000-nm
Payload: 2045-kg (4,500-lb) carried in internal weapons bays.
Engine: Pratt & Whitney F100-PW-220U
First Flight: 4 February 2011
Number of vehicles: 2

Boeing X-45C

Length: 39-ft overall; fuselage length 32-ft
Height: 4-ft
Span: 47-ft
Empty weight: 14,000-lb
Fuel volume: 5,400-lb
Payload: 4,500-lb (2041-kg)
Operating altitude: 40,000-ft
Cruise speed: Mach 0.85
Engine: General Electric F404-GE-102D
Radius: 1,300 nm

Boeing Phantom Ray

Length: 36 ft (10.9 m)
Wingspan: 50 ft (15.2 m)
Gross Weight: 36,500 lbs (16556 kg)
Operating Altitude: 40,000 ft (12192 m)
Cruise Mach: 0.8 (614 mph-988 km/h)
Engine: F404-GE-102D
First Flight: 27 April 2011

Chronology

April 1998: Phase One Technology Demonstration Contract was awarded
March 1999: Phase Two Technology Demonstration Contract was awarded
30 June 2000: DARPA and the USN awarded contracts for the first phase of the UCAV-N Advanced Technology Demonstrator program
September 2000: X-45A AV-1 was completed
September 2000: Block 1 software demonstrations completed
February 2001: Northrop Grumman formally unveiled the Pegasus design
16 June 2001: Pegasus officially designated X-47A at the Paris Air Salon
26 July 2001: Build 1.3-simulation demonstration.
7 August 2001: Spiral 1 award.
30 July 2001: The completed X-47 Pegasus was rolled out of its assembly hanger at Mojave, California
24 October 2001: X-45A AV-1 completes first low-speed taxi-test
December 2001: The X-47A conducted its first engine-run
20 April 2002: X-45A AV-1 completes first high-speed taxi-test
23 May 2002: X-45A AV-1 conducted its first flight
9 October 2002: Build 2.0-simulation demonstration
21 November 2002: The second X-45A, AV-2, completed its first flight
19 December 2002: The X-45A conducted the first flight with its undercarriage retracted and tack-off and landing from a hard surface runway
23 February 2003: The X-47A conducted its maiden flight.
28 February 2003: The X-45A completed Block 1 software demonstrations
3 November 2003: Block 2 software demonstrations commenced flight-testing on an X-45A
23 January 2004: An X-45A communicated with a manned T-33 UCAV surrogate in flight
20 March 2004: An X-45A dropped ordnance for the first time
18 April 2004: An X-45A dropped an inert GPS-guided bomb on a surface target
27 May 2004: Both X-45A's taxied together for the first time
2 August 2004: Both X-45A's demonstrated uninhabited coordinated flight
21 October 2004: X-45A block 3 software demonstrations commenced
10 November 2004: First engine for the X-45C was delivered to Boeing
9 December 2004: An X-45A conducted its first beyond-line-of-sight flight
27 January 2005: A transfer of command and control using line-of-sight of the 2 X-45A's was successfully demonstrated during Block 3 testing at Edwards AFB
4 February 2005: The 2 X-45A's flew a simulated combat mission, during which the programs 50th X-45 flight was achieved
13 May 2005: Boeing began flight-testing the Block 4 software during the 51st X-45A flight
August 2005: The final demonstration test series conducted during the 63rd and 64th X-45A flights
October 2006: The two X-45A's, after completing 64 flights between them, were allocated to the National Museum of the USAF at Wright Patterson AFB, Dayton Ohio and the Smithsonian National Air and Space Museum, Washington D.C.

Glossary

A	Attack
ACM	Advanced Cruise Missile
ACTIVE	Active Control Technology for Integrated Vehicles
AFB	Air Force Base
ATA	Advanced Tactical Aircraft
ATD	Advanced Technology Demonstration
ATF	Advanced Tactical Fighter
AV	Air Vehicle
BAe	British Aerospace
C	Cargo
DARPA	Defence Advanced Research Projects Agency
DFRC	Dryden Flight Research Centre
DoD	Department of Defence
F	Fighter
FATE	Future Aircraft Technology Enhancement
F/A	Fighter Attack
FBW	Fly By Wire
FCW	Flight Control System
FDL	Fighter Data Link
FWV	Fixed Wing Vehicle
GBU	Guided Bomb Unit
GPS	Global Positioning System
GVT	Ground Vibration Test
HiMAT	Highly Manoeuvrable Aircraft Technology
HMLV	Highly Manoeuvrable Lethal Vehicle
HUD	Heads Up Display
ICAV	Inhabited Combat Air Vehicle
ISR	Intelligence Surveillance and Reconnaissance
JDAM	Joint Direct Attack Munitions
JSAAWS	Joint-Semi-Autonomous Weapon System
J-UCAS	Joint Uninhabited Combat Air System
MCS	Mission Control Segment
MDC	McDonnell Douglas Corporation
MPAV	Multi-Purpose Air Vehicle
MQ	Armed Drone
NASA	National Aeronautical and Space Administration
NAVAIR	Naval Air Systems Command
NAWC-WD	Naval Air Warfare Centre-Weapons Division
NG	Northrop Grumman
RQ	Reconnaissance Drone
SATCOM	Satellite Communications
SDB	Small Diameter Bomb
SEC	Software Enabled Control
SEAD	Suppression of Enemy Air Defences
SRGPS	Shipboard Relative Global Positioning System
SSB	Small Smart Bomb
SSBN	Ballistic Missile Submarine
SSGN	Cruise Missile Submarine
STOL	Short Take-Off and Landing
T	Trainer
TLAM	Tomahawk Land Attack Missile
UAS	Unmanned Airborne System
UAV	Uninhabited Air Vehicle
UCAV	Uninhabited Combat Air Vehicle
UCAV-N	Uninhabited Combat Air Vehicle-Naval
UHF	Ultra High Frequency
UNSA	Uninhabited Naval Strike Aircraft
US	United States
USA	United States of America
USAF	United States Air Force
USN	United States Navy
VECTOR	Vectoring Extremely short take-off and landing Control and Tailless operation Research
VMC	Vehicle Management Computer
VTOL	Vertical Take-Off and Landing
VTUAV	Vertical Take-Off Uninhabited Air Vehicle
X	Experimental

Centurion Publishing

ISBN 10: 1-903630-21-5
ISBN 13: 978-1-903630-21-1

www.ingramcontent.com/pod-product-compliance
Lightning Source LLC
Chambersburg PA
CBHW081018040426
42444CB00014B/3257